Friendship
&
Faith

The WISDOM of Women
Creating Alliances for Peace

by the
Women of WISDOM

*Women's Interfaith Solutions for Dialogue and
Outreach in MetroDetroit*

Read The Spirit Books
an imprint of
David Crumm Media, LLC
Canton, Michigan

For more information and further discussion, visit

www.InterfaithWisdom.org

ISBN: 978-1-942011-93-4

Version 2.0

Cover art and design by Rick Nease

www.RickNeaseArt.com

Published By Read The Spirit Books
an imprint of David Crumm Media, LLC
42807 Ford Rd., Suite 234
Canton, Michigan, 48187 USA

Read The Spirit Books are produced by Front Edge Publishing, which specializes in speed and flexibility in adapting and updating our books. We can include links to video and other online media. We offer discounts on bulk purchases for special events, corporate training, and small groups. We are able to customize bulk orders by adding corporate or event logos on the cover and we can include additional pages inside describing your event or corporation. For more information about our fast and flexible publishing or permission to use our materials, please contact Front Edge Publishing at info@ FrontEdgePublishing.com.

Contents

WISDOM leaders who attended the annual banquet for the InterFaith Leadership Council of Metropolitan Detroit, where WISDOM was awarded the 2016 Interfaith Leadership award.

To all women, who hold the promise and power of relationship, and gift it to a world that still does not fully appreciate its potential. May these stories help to create space for peace, build bridges between individuals and communities, and create a more peaceful and just world—one relationship at a time.

Praise for Friendship & Faith

Quaker author Parker J. Palmer describes hope in this way: "Hope is holding in creative tension everything that is, with everything that could and should be, and every day taking action to lessen the distance between the two." I thought of this powerful description many times as I read the stories contained in Friendship & Faith. We are pressed daily by messages of fear, conflict and the idea that we are hopelessly divided by our differences. The stories contained in Friendship & Faith remind us of the richness and beauty contained in our diverse spiritual traditions, while affirming our shared human condition. These are the experiences of women and of the intimate connection between themselves, the stranger and the sacred. These are stories that present hospitality, generosity, courage, kindness, friendship and faithfulness as the visible expressions of invisible grace, grounded in hope that is gritty, visionary and accessible. What we need is right here, within us and between us, in the places we meet, in the moments we pray, in the times we reach out and across to one another in love.

From Carrie Newcomer, an internationally popular singer-songwriter and author who often collaborates in peacemaking efforts with Parker Palmer.

~

The stories in this book do more than tolerate other faiths and their practitioners. They celebrate and embrace friends bound together on a spiritual path. There is no "in" and no "out." Only together.

From Maggie Rowe, a popular writer for TV series (including *Arrested Development*) whose critically acclaimed memoir *Sin Bravely* describes her own struggle to overcome the religious rigidity of her own upbringing.

I couldn't put the book down. I suddenly realized that tears were streaming down my face. I was so moved as I read about the personal experiences of women having immigrated to the United States, of moving from place to place, of encountering unfamiliar people, practices and rituals. And, I was struck by what these stories have in common; how each of them found a friend, someone who could simply hold a hand, share a story, or help out from time to time. I hope the stories in this book remind us of the value of friendship. I hope they encourage us to reach out to the person sitting alone, knock on a neighbor's door, welcome the newcomer into our communities and our lives.

From Rabbi Marla R. Hornsten of Temple Israel in Michigan, North America's largest Reform Jewish congregation.

～

These precise kinds of stories are so important! Too many voices of strength and privilege, right now, are urging us to defend, isolate, protect and deride—and are telling us that differences matter more than similarities. Ultimately, these voices are telling us that anxiety should motivate instead of love. It is my prayer that this book will contribute to the voices of love and hope and friendship that still are calling us to courageously cross lines in love.

From Adey Wassink, author and senior pastor of the Iowa-based Sanctuary Community Church, part of the nationwide Blue Ocean Faith movement of congregations that promote inclusivity.

～

In a time when divisions between people seem to be widening, Friendship & Faith brings hope and inspiration. One person connecting with the heart of another makes a difference. Sharing stories is a powerful way to bring hope and transformation. Scientists are finding that the human need for connection is as critical as the need for food and water. Yet, in our ever-changing world, many struggle to find that connection. Reading the stories of these courageous women, who are willing to look deep and see the spirit that connects us all, sparked a feeling in me to step outside and take a chance to say: "Hello."

From Christine Zimmerman, LMSW, a social worker, educator and author whose goal is "creating a peaceful, joyful space where growth happens and spirit blossoms."

∼

In recent years, my weekly column has been called GodSigns, exploring the many ways God is continually connecting our lives, so the themes in Friendship & Faith run throughout my own work as a writer. In Jewish tradition, the Torah commands us to fulfill the concept of tikkun olam, or making the world a better place. Friendship is a current beneath the surface of our lives that buoys us and keeps us moving forward—together. Friendship is a way that, every day, each one of us can help to reconnect our broken world.

From Suzy Farbman, a nationally known columnist and author who has written for many newspapers and national magazines throughout her career. Her latest memoir *GodSigns* is also the title of her weekly columns at *ReadTheSpirit.com* online magazine.

Foreword

By Barbara Mahany

Day after day I wake up with my chest feeling hollowed. The space in my heart hurts so much, so immeasurably, I can't fathom how to contain it. I shuffle down the stairs of my old shingled house, look out the windows into the quiet of dawn, into the leafy arbors, and wonder how in the world can I stitch a single thread into the tatters of this world, this oozing brokenness all around?

I walk in a state of grief unlike any I've ever known—and I've known quite a few. My grief is for the state of this nation, for the body politic, for the sheer goodness and kindness that I see being battered day after day. I shrink from the modern-day public square—social media in all its iterations—because the vitriol is too much, because the divisiveness tears me apart. I don't believe in a world of us versus them, and yet, every day those lines are drawn more starkly. I cling to the words of wise souls like Father Jim Martin, the Jesuit thinker and author, who writes from his Christian perspective: "For with Jesus, there is no us and them. There is only us."

But how, I keep wondering, can my one all-alone voice make a dent in the cacophony? How can a whisper be heard? How can I amplify my deep faith in bridging, not burning? Where oh where is there a place for a soul who believes so deeply, yet finds herself flailing with so little a footprint?

And then, the stories of this book landed on my desk. *This*, I knew right away, is where the answer lies: In ordinary-extraordinary stories of women who reach across doorways, and hallways, and kitchen counters—who see beyond burkas and veils and prayer beads and venerations. I see and I read and I wrap myself in the stories of human hearts reaching beyond their own private shelters—walls that, always, can go one of two ways: to open into doorways, or seal themselves off, barricades of hard stubborn coldness, otherness, unwilling-to-bend-ness.

Here, in the pages of this book, is the first best draft of humanity moving forward. Here are the blueprints for the great and eternal commandment: Love as you would be loved.

Here is Ayesha, alone and with newborn babe, falling into the bottomless shadow of post-partum depression, who dared to knock on the door across the hall, and found a friend—and earthly salvation—in the form of an elderly widow named Libby. The Indian Muslim new mother befriending the white Christian widow; both finding the solace they sought—in each other. As we read, we join her in the suspense of that simple, daring act: raising a fist to a door—and knocking. The toeholds of courage start small.

Here is Parwin, who recounts the hair-raising story of her escape, while six months pregnant, from war-ravaged Afghanistan during the Soviet-Afghan war. With two young children in tow, and determined to keep their escape unnoticed, she and her troupe traveled by truck and by horse and by foot—150 miles of fear beyond fear. And in the end, when she delivered that baby just across the Pakistani border, when she found her way to America, she devoted her life to justice, compassion, for living the words of the blessed Qur'an: ...*that you may know each other—and not despise each other.*

Here is Dolores, who says she was "marinated, battered and deep-fried in religion," specifically the black Baptist religion of her youth, and who found herself drawn into a host of houses of worship—mosques, synagogues, churches large and loud or not-so-large and not-so-loud. She was drawn, in particular, to the Buddhist practice of silence—a far cry from the joyful noise of her youth. One night, after a long dry spell in the faith department, she dreamed that Jesus introduced her to his best friend Buddha. Ever since, she's been a practicing Buddhist. And even more so, a living, breathing bridge between two of the world's great religions.

Story after story, woman after woman, the leitmotif is always: Reach beyond what you know. Reach into the unknown, the foreign, the mysterious. Make it yours through words, and gesture, and deep human touch. Defy the divisiveness. Believe in the power of your own still small voice.

I turn to the holy wisdom of Dorothy Day, who learned from Therese of Lisieux: "By little and by little"—by little acts of kindness, by little acts of courage—we can thread the needle that will stitch the tatters back into wholeness.

We cannot afford to shrink from the task. We cannot afford to think we don't matter, that we can't make a difference. Read these stories of oversize courage and unbounded goodness. Read these stories of faith and justice, doled out in everyday measure.

Be the change you believe in. Be the kindness. Be the radiant light.

Go now, and carve out heaven on earth.

Barbara Mahany is an author and for nearly 30 years wrote for the Chicago Tribune. Before that, she was a pediatric oncology nurse at Children's Memorial Hospital in Chicago. Her books *Motherprayer* and *Slowing Time* bring together many spiritual threads from a lifetime of experiences with families.

Preface

By Eileen Flanagan

As the stories in this volume show, friendships across difference can open our eyes and hearts. They can break through loneliness, grief, and prejudice, leading to a new or deeper sense of connection. They can provide a balm in a wounded world, inspiring our work to heal it. They have done all of these in my own life, which is why I am happy to be part of *Friendship & Faith*. For me, these two transforming elements of my life have been deeply intertwined.

I've been blessed, not only with the adventure of exploring friends' food, culture or religious practice, but also with the challenge of helping them to understand my own. Explaining Catholic Mass to a Jewish friend who came with me one Sunday during Second Grade forced me to ask myself for the first time, "Why do we stand, sit or kneel at particular moments in the liturgy?" Childhood friendships across lines of race made me question the prejudices of my Irish family and taught me "that of God" resides in all people, a core tenant of the Quaker faith I adopted as an adult.

As a Peace Corps Volunteer in Botswana in my 20s, I had to answer questions about the United States, such as, "Is it true that you send your elders away from their families?" Living in an African village, where such a separation was unthinkable, made me see my own individualistic culture with new eyes. Being the only woman among a teaching staff of men, I was especially grateful to find a female friend to tutor me in Tswana language and culture. Mmadithapelo Ditirwa explained the Tswana proverb "*Motho ke motho ka botho*" ("A person is a person because of other people") and the ethic of reciprocity it implied. She taught me to *boladisa*, to walk my guest half way home, whether that was a few meters or a few kilometers.

Twenty-five years later, it was my friendship with Mmadithapelo that motivated a major change in my life. After many years and the development of cell phones, we had reconnected and had started calling each other periodically. One time I asked about the weather—an innocent Botswana pastime—and learned how rising heat and erratic rain were affecting subsistence farmers. I had been concerned about climate change before that, but when I started researching the horrific predictions for Africa, I knew I had to do more than composting my banana peels and taking short showers. Thinking of Mmaditapelo's children, Mopati and Tshego, I joined a group that used nonviolent direct action to address climate justice, a step that led to a new career: training people in nonviolent methods of making change.

I believe more than ever, "A person is a person because of other people." It's never been clearer that our survival as a species depends on our seeing our commonality, on our ability to reach across our differences and work together for the world we want to see—for our own and for each others children. As many faith traditions teach, we are ultimately all One.

And yet I've come to realize that there is a blind spot that can form among spiritual white people like myself if we focus exclusively on our common experiences and interests without recognizing the pain of the separation the world inflicts upon us. I learned this lesson from a friend, of course—a gay black man named Matthew Armstead. Matthew and I had attended an environmental justice rally, where speakers stressed the high asthma rates in low-income communities of color. Near the end, a rabbi said, "We are all one," and afterwards I told Matthew it was my favorite of the speeches.

"I hated that speech," he said with more emotion than I expected.

Matthew had recently spent three weeks supporting young activists in Ferguson, MO, after Darren Wilson, a white cop, shot to death Michael Brown, an unarmed black teenager. Brown's body had been left in the street for hours, sparking national outrage. Days before the environmental justice rally, a grand jury had exonerated Wilson, reinforcing the feeling that black lives really didn't matter to white America. On the way home from the rally Matthew explained, "We may all be one, but we're not exactly experiencing the world that way at the moment."

In the years since this incident, I've become convinced that Matthew's insight is crucial. We are all one—but we're not experiencing the world that way at the moment. Saying both affirms the spiritual truth without erasing the experience of people who are being treated as "other" in the here and now, an erasure that can undermine trust and true friendship.

To work effectively for peace and justice, we need to acknowledge both levels of reality, or we won't be able to bridge the differences that are cynically used to divide us. This is one reason why people of faith have a special role to play. Our diverse traditions give us tools to bridge the gap between how we are called to live and how we actually do live. They give us language for human failings and hope for human redemption, while reminding us that we are all ultimately—*One*.

Our friendships across difference can be potent teachers of both our common humanity and the ways our experiences of the world differ profoundly. The stories in this volume are a reminder of both and a blueprint for reaching out across the chasms through the simple human act of becoming a friend.

Eileen Flanagan is an award-winning author of three books. She has emerged as a leader in the climate justice movement, a story told in her memoir, *Renewable: One Woman's Search for Simplicity, Faithfulness, and Hope*. She also has been sharing what she has learned about effective and spiritually grounded activism through her online course, *We Were Made for this Moment*. She is a Quaker based in Philadelphia.

Introduction

By Patricia Montemurri

Ask my daughter, a recent college graduate, about the catch phrases she heard from me growing up. When she spotted a schoolmate or a familiar face, and balked at acknowledging them, I'd urge her to try this.

"Just say, 'Hi!' "

As basic as my advice may have been back then, we have reached an era when simple hospitality across racial, cultural and religious lines is rare. This book is about all the good we can accomplish by simply greeting each other. Like the coaching I once gave my daughter, this book is the call to action we all need now as adults: Just be friendly. That's the advice of the women who make up WISDOM, a Michigan-based, decade-old organization of women from multiple religious faiths.

You probably picked up this book because you are captivated by all those faces and those smiles on the cover. And because you're curious. Thanks to God, Yahweh, Allah, Buddha and to all other heavenly forces that these women were curious, too, about each other's religious traditions and inspirations. Thanks for the heart, gumption, faith, wit, warmth and wisdom they are sharing in these 52 stories.

WISDOM started after Gail Katz, who is Jewish; Trish Harris, who is Catholic; Shahina Begg, who converted to Islam from Hinduism; and Peggy Kalis, who belonged to the Unity Church, met over informal lunches to discuss the underpinnings of their faith. Together they formed the Women's Interfaith Solutions for Dialogue and Outreach in Metro Detroit, aka WISDOM. Over the past decade, the non-profit WISDOM has presented and co-sponsored more than 100 public programs in and out of

Michigan, highlighted by women sharing stories of friendship that cross divisions created by the imagined barriers of religion. I first encountered them as a journalist for the Detroit Free Press, and asked the founding members about New Year's tips for spiritual renewal.

They teach that the Golden Rule is universal across faiths. As important as what people believe is how they behave. Show me; don't tell me.

One of WISDOM's first outreach programs was to make aid packages for children affected by war in Sudan's Darfur region in 2006. As they filled each package, they asked participants to recite a tenet from the dozen faiths represented in the room about how to love your neighbor as yourself.

In 2009, WISDOM produced a book called *Friendship & Faith*, filled with 29 stories from women representing eight religious faiths, describing how they crossed barriers to find friendship on the other side. More women have joined them in recent years. They've got more stories to tell now. At a time when our nation's leaders often promote divisive rhetoric and raises global barriers, WISDOM women are doubling down on the power of a hello and the ensuing conversation, education, illumination and inclusion. When the appeal to expand *Friendship & Faith* with new stories first went out through the WISDOM network a year ago, leaders expected that a few courageous women would step forward. Instead, they were overwhelmed when two dozen women produced deeply inspiring true stories that circle the globe. Then, in the weeks before publication, even more women—including famous authors nationwide—stepped forward to add their names and voices to this expanded book.

That remarkable outpouring of support demonstrates, once again, that women's leadership builds healthy communities and, most importantly, compassionate communities. At a time of escalating political polarity, disinformation and hate speech, it is vital to nurture interfaith relationships that teach us not only about the truths of other faiths and cultures—but deepen our awareness of compassionate truths in our own traditions. Many of the women in these pages point out that their new friendships did more than expand their knowledge of other cultures— and, along the way, help them feel more comfortable in their diverse communities. These new friendships opened their eyes to the compassionate depth and breadth of their own religious traditions.

And, in that truth, I recognized my own story. I grew up the eldest daughter of Italian immigrants. I was schooled in the rigid teachings of the time—that Roman Catholicism was the one true faith. I was a bit of a skeptic even in 3rd grade, when my image of a benevolent God didn't square with the instruction that unbaptized children in faraway places were doomed without the money I contributed to missions for the care and baptism of so-called "pagan babies."

Throughout my long career as a journalist, reporting on an amazingly diverse corner of the world in southeast Michigan, I found my own understanding of Catholicism broadening. I wrote many stories about Catholic women religious. I discovered that the founders and leaders of the congregations of nuns who taught me were some of the first advocates of women's empowerment. Today, we'd call them the early feminists, even if the term would have seemed foreign to them. With courage and remarkable fortitude, they built the first schools and hospitals in many communities. They put their faith into action around the world.

In the women of WISDOM, I see the shared values that underscore my upbringing.

May you make the same discoveries in these pages.

Patricia Montemurri is a Michigan-based journalist who was a staff writer at the Detroit Free Press for nearly 37 years. She covered a wide range of issues and personalities, from presidents to popes and Miss America contestants. Her specialties included women's issues and coverage of the Catholic Church. She is the author of *Detroit Gesu Catholic Church and School*, a book that explores the history of a landmark church in a diverse community within Detroit.

Part I

Forming the Circle

This book is about making and keeping friends.

As leaders of WISDOM, we spent a long time talking with women from a range of cultural and professional backgrounds, asking a wide-open question: What could we offer in a book that would help women improve their own lives—and build stronger communities in the process?

The answer came back in a chorus: Give us a book about real people daring to cross boundaries to make friends. Tell us how they did it. Tell us why they needed a friend. Tell us about their best ideas for encouraging friendships in the larger community. Tell us about their anxieties as they reached out. Tell us some dramatic stories—but also tell us some ordinary, everyday stories about ordinary people, just like us.

CHAPTER 1

WISDOM Co-Founders
Forming the Circle

*There is something distinctive about how women work
together. We tend to take the time to build the relationships
first, and then work on solving the problem.*
—Trish Harris

Gail Katz is Jewish, Shahina Begg is Muslim and Patricia "Trish" Harris is Catholic. Gail and Shahina contributed individual stories for this book. All three met and became friends through connections with the innovative interfaith project called "The Children of Abraham," developed by Brenda Rosenberg, whose story also appears in this volume.

As we open this collection of stories about friendship and faith, Gail, Shahina and Trish talk about how their friendships evolved and expanded into an organization: WISDOM (Women's Interfaith Solutions for Dialogue and Outreach in MetroDetroit, www. interfaithwisdom.org). As you enjoy their story, you will find themes that will echo as you read the personal stories in this book. In the end, the creative work of an organization like WISDOM is possible only through a wide network of relationships.

GAIL: This story begins at a time when each of us had our own reasons why we were attracted to forming a women's interfaith group but, although each of us had had those reasons for a number of years, we hadn't really been acting on them. In fact, we might never have even met had it not been for the Children of Abraham Project.

I got involved with Children of Abraham back when it was in the form of a play, performed in various places. As an educator, I had been involved in diversity programs for young people for years. I had seen the play quite early on at the Jewish Ensemble Theater in the West Bloomfield Jewish Community Center, and I was just blown away by it, which is why I agreed to be a facilitator for students. After these performances, I worked with groups of middle-school students, talking about what they had just experienced.

TRISH: The play is part of my story, too. I'd saved the playbill from my first experience viewing the Children of Abraham show in 2004, because I was so powerfully moved by it. You know, it's entirely possible that, over the years, the three of us may have attended some of the same events, but we never met until 2006.

SHAHINA: I do recall seeing Gail much earlier, at an interfaith event where she was leading a group of students, but I didn't formally meet her then.

My own interfaith journey, like so many of the women in WISDOM, goes back a very long way. In my life, it goes back to my childhood in India and to marrying my husband, Victor, who is Muslim. I had grown up Hindu and converted to Islam in 1975. Victor and I always were interested in interfaith work. When Brenda Rosenberg was first creating the Children of Abraham production, our daughter, Sofia, agreed to help Brenda in writing parts of what became the final play. So I always felt very close to that play and attended performances whenever I could.

Later, there was a documentary film created about the whole Children of Abraham process. Brenda invited me to come and see the documentary when it was shown for the first time at Kirk in the Hills Church in Bloomfield Hills, Michigan. This was the spring of 2006, and I excitedly accepted the invitation. I have always been interested in visiting various places of worship, and as I had often driven past this beautiful church, I was especially looking forward to this event.

GAIL: We all had been involved in some way with diversity initiatives, but we did not get to know one another before that event at Kirk in the Hills. In fact, I didn't actually meet Trish that night, but our connections began there.

TRISH: I was there that night at the Kirk. I had read about the premiere in my church's bulletin and, remembering the play from almost two years before, I was eager to see the documentary. I was so impressed by the play that I actually bought eight extra tickets so some of my friends could attend the documentary showing. That night at the Kirk was an important moment because it brought together hundreds of people who were interested in this kind of work—many for the first time.

GAIL: I did meet Shahina that night. I had already met her husband, Victor, at various interfaith events, but I had never had a chance to meet his wife. That evening I also met Peggy Kalis, who would become a co-founder of WISDOM, but who has since moved out of the Metro Detroit area. At that time, Peggy Kalis was a member of a local Unity church and was very active in interfaith work.

SHAHINA: There was a "talk back" opportunity after the Children of Abraham documentary was shown that night. I was so inspired after seeing the documentary and hearing the responses from the participants in that debriefing session.

During the reception that followed the event, I had a conversation with Barbara Clevenger, who is a Unity minister. I said, "Wouldn't it be nice for women of many faith traditions to work together in the same way that the teens in the Children of Abraham project collaborated together in the making of their theatrical production, but with an emphasis on things like community service projects?"

Barbara said, "Let me introduce you to someone who would be very interested in this idea." She introduced me to Peggy Kalis and, right away, something clicked. I remember that Peggy talked to me about a visit she had made to an open house at a mosque in Canton, Michigan. She had taken part in some prayers there and had had a very positive experience. She said that she wanted to work on more opportunities like this for women, and I knew immediately that we had a lot in common.

GAIL: At the end of the Kirk program, there was a social time for chatting and eating. My husband and I began talking with other Jewish folks we knew, and we might have visited only with those friends that night. But, the next thing I knew, this complete stranger—Peggy Kalis—came right up to me. I think someone had pointed me out to her in the crowd, because of my educational work in diversity.

Peggy said, "Perhaps you might be interested in putting together an initiative to get women together to talk about their faith traditions like the young adults have done in the Children of Abraham Project."

My first reaction was: No way! I'm already running the Religious Diversity Journeys for seventh-graders in Oakland County. I'm already the chair of the annual World Sabbath service, an interfaith event that focuses on youth. I was doing so much already. How could I take on another committee? That's what I thought this was—just another committee forming.

I didn't say it that way to Peggy, though. I listened to her politely. I felt tense as she began to talk about this. After a while—and maybe she sensed what I was feeling—she finally said, "How about if we just meet for coffee?"

I agreed to that with some reservations, thinking that this was as far as I'd let this relationship go.

Then, I talked with Shahina that evening as well, and I began to think: You know, this really is right up my alley—women reaching out to other women who might not get to meet one another because of close-knit circles of friends and family members within their own faith traditions.

TRISH: The documentary premiere was only the start of this effort toward interfaith dialogue. Meanwhile, four local places of worship had committed to hosting a day during the following month for people who wanted to experience their worship service, ask questions and enjoy refreshments and fellowship afterwards. Kirk in the Hills, the Muslim Unity Center, Temple Beth El and St. Hugo of the Hills Catholic Church all participated. I wanted to attend all four congregations, but was out of town for the weekends that the mosque and the temple held their programs. I was able to attend the ones at Kirk and St. Hugo's. It was at St. Hugo's that I met Shahina.

SHAHINA: That was a wonderful event! After the Mass, there was a question-and-answer session. This was my first time at a Catholic church, and it provided me an opportunity to clarify some of the questions I had. Interfaith gatherings like these begin to break down our stereotypes and misunderstandings so that our conversations can begin to flow openly.

TRISH: After the Q&A session, we all walked down to the parish hall to enjoy a buffet and some further discussion. I was one of the first to arrive, and I'd decided to sit at an empty table, hoping that people I didn't know might join me. An imam, Victor, and Shahina sat down at my table, and I spent the rest of the afternoon talking with Shahina.

SHAHINA: We had such a nice conversation that day. We started out talking about our backgrounds and then ventured on to other topics. I don't think Trish had met that many Muslims before that point, had you?

TRISH: No, up to this time I had only casual professional acquaintances with Muslims at work, but I hadn't really interacted with Muslims socially or discussed their faith with them.

SHAHINA: At St. Hugo's that day, I remember we talked for quite a while. It was very casual and comfortable. This was the same way I had felt when I met Gail for the first time. We hit it off immediately.

TRISH: I told Shahina: "I'm sorry that I missed the program at the Muslim Unity Center."

She said, "Don't feel bad! We're having an Open House. Come to our Open House!"

SHAHINA: That's right! I invited you to the mosque that day.

TRISH: But before the date of that Open House at the Muslim Unity Center, there was one more service in the series, at Kirk in the Hills. I attended that event and, once again, I ended up connecting with Shahina. She repeated her invitation to come to the Open House at her mosque. This additional meeting was important, because as the date for the Open House drew nearer, I had begun to get cold feet. I wanted to go, but was a little afraid of going alone into an unknown environment. My curiosity and the rapport that had built up between Shahina and me gave me the "push" I needed to attend. Getting to know this one person opened the door for me to expand my worldview.

SHAHINA: We had spent so much time planning for that special day at the Unity Center! We wanted to teach people about the history of Islam, but we also wanted them to feel welcome and to simply get to know us. Our hope was to live up to the Unity Center's founding values of unity and diversity, by bringing people of varying ethnic and cultural backgrounds together.

TRISH: That Open House was so much fun. I thought I'd be there for maybe 40 minutes, but ended up staying for three hours. Once again, I saw Shahina right away, and she began introducing me to more people. I ended up doing everything the hosts had planned. I toured the mosque, saw a video on Islam, had my picture taken in a "desert" tent, collected pamphlets on Islam and ate wonderful Middle Eastern food.

As I was getting ready to leave the mosque, I saw Shahina and sat down for a moment to thank her for a wonderful afternoon. During the course of my goodbye, I shared something with her that had been on my mind for some time. This was sparked by my experience with the original play and by my participation in the Children of Abraham project over the last month—a desire to do something together as "Women of Abraham."

I remember Shahina looking at me and saying, "Funny you should mention that. Two other women are interested in doing something like that as well. Would you like to join us for coffee?"

GAIL: What Trish didn't know is that this was the coffee date that we had planned way back at the Kirk. I knew that I was planning to have coffee with Peggy and Shahina, but then this fourth woman showed up, whom I didn't know at all: Trish.

That coffee date turned out to be the key moment when all four of the WISDOM co-founders were together for the first time!

TRISH: It's likely that we had been in the same crowd together somewhere previously, but this was the first time that we had knowingly been together—all four of us around the table for conversation.

GAIL: From the start, we didn't do much with the "Women of Abraham" phrase, because we didn't want to limit the group to women from the Abrahamic faiths: Judaism, Christianity and Islam. We wanted to be open to Hindus, Jains and others, too.

TRISH: That was an eye-opener for me. What I had experienced so far was the Children of Abraham approach, including only the "People of the Book": Jews, Christians and Muslims. The other women had a much broader vision. Our scope came to include any and all women, regardless of faith tradition, and including those of no faith tradition. As we talked more, it became clear to me that I was the "novice" in interfaith matters. Gail had "lived" interfaith for much of her life, and was sincerely devoted to repairing the world. Shahina had an international background and had been instrumental in the founding of a mosque that brought Muslims of different ethnic and national backgrounds together. Peggy worked for a Christian faith-based organization and had many ties to various charities. I was a little overwhelmed by my lack of experience, knowledge and networking in inter-faith work.

SHAHINA: That first meeting was important, but it wasn't an ideal setting. There were a lot of people there in that coffee shop—a lot of noise. It wasn't a good place to talk too much about our lives.

GAIL: I could see that, too, and finally I said, "You know what? Let's make a dinner date at my house where we really can talk. We can spend hours, if we want."

Our coffee meeting was in May of 2006 and, that same month, the four of us met at my home for dinner. We set no agenda that night. I suppose that if men are talking about an idea for a new organization, they may start with an agenda before they do anything else. But what women do is sit down around a table and start talking.

That's what we did. We didn't have any formal plan. We began sharing and soon, we were speaking from the heart with one another.

SHAHINA: Everyone was so open and candid. We delved straight into some deep questions. "What's your story?" "Where do you come from?" "What's your history?"

GAIL: "What are your interests?" "Tell us about your children." "Do you have a significant other?" "What challenges do you have in your life now?" "Where have you traveled?" "Where have you worked?" "What's really important to you in your faith tradition?" We connected on all kinds of levels. We talked and talked—and talked—that night.

We did conclude with: "What should we do now?" But nearly all of the evening was spent sharing our personal stories honestly with one another.

SHAHINA: There was no leader in that circle. We each told our stories as equals.

GAIL: We must have spent at least three or four hours with one another. We weren't thinking of the time. It just flew by.

SHAHINA: At that point, we weren't even thinking about the specific details of the project itself. That wasn't as important as getting to know one another, first.

GAIL: The four of us must have met four or five times before we ever got down to talking about specific details of a program.

Finally, we agreed that we all wanted to bring more women together. For that, we needed an event—an opportunity for more women to form relationships, like we were doing. Our first meetings together were in the spring of 2006 and we planned our first large event for that August.

That's when we turned to a detailed planning process. That's also when we began to realize how important this work was. That was the summer of the Israel-Hezbollah War. My husband and I went on a vacation at the end of July, and I took my laptop along and checked in on my interfaith work. Soon, I was reading emails firing back and forth between Jews and Muslims over the war, and it was very heated. Some of the exchanges were downright ugly. I was beginning to pull my hair out with concern and total frustration.

I remember one prominent religious leader saying: "I am no longer going to be involved in interfaith programs"—and he left a group where he'd played an important role. He just pulled out, because he felt that he could not interact with the local Muslims. I was horrified.

We already had our first WISDOM program on the docket. When I got home from the vacation, I thought: Look what's going on in the world! Look what's happening with relationships in our own community! I was so distraught.

Our first large event was on August 20, 2006. We had invited women to work together on a local Habitat for Humanity building site. We had no idea what to expect.

TRISH: This was our first event. I was excited and scared. Would people actually show up? Would they work together? Would our opening ceremony touch people and not turn them off? Would our icebreakers work during the lunch break? Would the participants have enough time to get to know one another? Would they feel that they had done something meaningful for themselves and for the community?

SHAHINA: That day, we were scheduled to work on installing windows and siding on two homes. Most of the women who had signed up had no experience with construction, so we were all a little nervous about who would show up.

GAIL: From this first event—and continuing with every other interfaith initiative that we've put together in WISDOM—we've committed ourselves to very careful planning. We work hard on this. People have to register. We make sure people will be comfortable. We ensure that people will interact with folks of different faith traditions.

Still, we all were blown away at the Habitat site when 55 women actually showed up. With everything else going on in the world, with some skepticism from other people about what we were doing—they came!

TRISH: We started that day in a park near the homes where we would be working. We formed a big circle of women and we had several different people offer prayers from their different faith traditions. Those opening prayers set the intention for the entire day. After we explained how the day would unfold, the Habitat for Humanity staff briefed us on the different jobs that we could perform throughout the day.

GAIL: We had planned the whole day. Big sheets were laid out on the grass for the women to sit on during the lunch break. We structured the break so that all the Christians didn't wind up in one corner and all the Muslims in another corner.

We provided them with icebreaker questions. We usually do that in our events, because it's too easy to fall into talking about something like—you know, what's on TV that week. So, we provide questions to help get the conversations going in a meaningful direction. We might ask: "How did you get your name?" "What does your name mean?" "What's your most prized possession?" "What's a family tradition within your religion that you participate in each year?"

That day at the Habitat site, with all of those women sitting down to lunch—we could tell it was working when the volume of conversation began to rise everywhere. We actually had women telling us they wanted more time to talk, and were reluctant to break off the conversations to go back to work.

TRISH: But the women were also very committed to the work we had gathered to accomplish that day. When we had to call a halt to the construction, clean up the site and put away the tools, everyone was so involved with this joint initiative that no one wanted to stop. The evaluations indicated that the women were proud of what they were able to accomplish, and the only negative comment related to wanting more time to do more work on the houses together.

GAIL: At the end of the day, we came back together and formed our big circle again. We sang a Beatles song.

TRISH: We sang *Give Peace a Chance.*

GAIL: I know this was a Beatles song—and that may sound odd. It wasn't a traditional faith-based song. But I couldn't help but to get all choked up in that circle, singing that song, and I know I wasn't the only one who felt that way. We were so connected that day. We had done something that was useful. We had helped two families who needed these homes. We had come together as women from many different faiths and we had gotten to know one another through the whole experience. We connected at a deep, spiritual level.

TRISH: There had been a lot of pre-event apprehension. But as the day progressed, there was a palpable feeling of confidence that arose among us. The all-women crew—most of which had little or no construction experience—was able, with direction from the Habitat staff, to contribute significantly to the construction projects. The women's overwhelmingly positive approval of the event, their desire to be included in future events and the friendships made that day showed us that we could organize a successful interfaith event—and our confidence grew.

GAIL: That's a central part of everything we do together— empowering women to do new things!

I've been involved in interfaith work for years, but WISDOM has changed my life. I've grown a great deal in at least two areas. One of the areas involves organizational skills, and much of what I've learned is from working with my buddy, Trish. Through this work together, I've helped to organize all kinds of educational events and community service projects. I am the president of WISDOM and have a board of directors consisting of women of eight different religions, which includes an executive board, and

I've learned a lot about what really works when you're trying to bring people together to make a difference in your community.

The other major change in my life is my deep desire to learn more about my own Jewish tradition. I have been very committed to furthering my Jewish education, and it has become very clear to me that I have a burning desire to connect with my own Judaism on a very spiritual level. In getting to know this diverse group of women, I've deepened my own faith.

TRISH: The same thing has happened to me. Skills I used in my professional career have been directly applicable to the founding and development of WISDOM, and the programs we have coordinated. I have also developed some new skills that would never have come about otherwise. My WISDOM interactions and friendships have challenged me to re-examine my own faith in an effort to explain it to others. My faith and worldview have been both deepened and expanded.

SHAHINA: I've experienced the same thing. I realized that I didn't know as much as I should know about Islam. Anytime people would ask me questions, I was hesitant to answer because I wasn't sure I was giving an accurate answer. I've signed up for classes, too, to learn more about Islam, and I really look forward to them.

My friendship with Gail, Trish, Peggy and others has deepened the spirituality in so many aspects of my life. I realize that amidst all of the planning and coordinating and organizational work that we do, what I really value most is the bond that we have built. I truly cherish the knowledge that no matter what is going on in the world, that I have these friends upon whom I can rely.

TRISH: In the end, everything we've done through WISDOM begins with faith and with the relationships we have been able to build together.

There is something distinctive, generally speaking, about how women work together. We tend to take the time to build the relationships first, and then work on solving the problem. When we add faith to those relationships, we find that it gives us the strength needed to deepen our understanding of, our respect for and our connections with one another. Men generally begin by trying to resolve the issue—often without initially building the relationships that make resolution more probable.

GAIL: Our goal is not to solve the Middle East problem or to get involved with worldwide political differences. We are trying to break down barriers, to increase respect and understanding, and to dispel myths and stereotypes here, locally, in Metro Detroit. We have learned that we can change lives, strengthen our community and be a model for others, if we don't lose sight of the fact that this process begins by forming relationships—one friend at a time!

Part II

Making Friends

Friendship is richer when we discover it on the other side of a barrier we did not expect to cross.

CHAPTER 2

Azar Alizadeh
A Friendship Despite a Secret

This just doesn't make sense!" I said. It seemed so unfair.

Azar was born in Iran and is a fourth-generation Baháʼí. She has been a U.S. citizen since 1975 and, in recent years, has hosted a weekly public-television program in Michigan, called *Interfaith Odyssey.*

WHEN I WAS growing up, my best friend kept a secret from me for a long time. I grew up on the north side of Tehran, Iran, in a happy family. My father had a store that sold imported fabrics from Europe. Our house was made up of two flats; we lived downstairs, and my aunt lived upstairs.

Most of the people in Iran are Muslim, but I grew up around people of other faiths as well. There were some Jewish people, some Zoroastrians and I am a fourth-generation Bahá'í. In the 1950s—under the Shah, things were not easy for Bahá'ís—but conditions were not as bad as they became later. We heard the Shah had a doctor who was Bahá'í.

We felt secure, even though sometimes bad things happened. In my third-grade class in the public school, I was singled out by a teacher who asked Bahá'í students to raise their hands. I know three of us in that class were Bahá'í, but I wasn't as smart as the others. I actually raised my hand. The teacher singled me out to go sit in the corner, and she punished me by saying that I had to hold one of my feet off the floor for a while. All of this only because I was Bahá'í.

Later, my parents moved me to a private school. My best friend through these years was named Tahmineh, a Muslim girl whose family lived near mine in Tehran. She had a very good sense of humor, and I did, too. We became best friends and we often walked back and forth to school together, or sometimes took a bus.

Tahmineh and I were selected by the producer of a national radio show who was looking for children to appear in weekly broadcasts from Tehran—so that was something else I shared with Tahmineh. This was a children's program that aired every Friday, which is like Sunday in the U.S. It was an idea similar to *Sesame Street*. These were not religious broadcasts, but just nice weekly stories for children with good lessons behind them. Every week there was a different story about 20 or 25 minutes long. The children who worked with the show each played a part in telling the story. The director and producer would meet with us to show us our parts so we could practice. It was a lot of fun. I had a great-aunt who lived far away from us, but she would say, "Every

Friday, I can turn on the radio and know that you are doing well, because I hear your voice on the radio!"

Tahmineh and I spent a lot of time together. There was no way, just by looking at us, that one could tell that Tahmineh was Muslim and I was Bahá'í. We wore the same kinds of clothes. During the Shah's regime, women did not cover their hair as much.

We visited each other's homes. At first, we played together. As we got older, we read books together or listened to the radio. We'd spend an hour or two together visiting like this in our homes. Eventually I began to notice that, when I visited Tahmineh's house, her mother would give us things to eat, but I could not recall Tahmineh eating anything at my house.

One day, when we were about 12 or 13, I visited her house and her mother gave me something good to eat. This time, I said, "Tahmineh never eats at our house."

There was silence. They didn't say anything. I knew that there was something they did not want to talk about, so I let the subject drop.

The next day when Tahmineh and I were walking to school, I asked, "Why is it that you never eat our food? Don't you like our food? When I asked about this yesterday at your house, no one answered me."

Again, there was silence. We had never talked about this before. Finally, she said, "It's a secret."

"A secret?" I said, "Tell me! Tell me!"

Then she explained, "My parents say that Bahá'ís put things in their food and drink that will make other people become Bahá'í."

I didn't cry, but this hurt me; we were just children, and this was painful. I told her: "Tahmineh! This is just a myth!"

The secret was out and, as we talked, we both understood what had happened. There was a fanatical mullah (an Islamic clergyman) who was spreading hatred against Bahá'ís across the country. One of the myths that he was spreading was this claim that Bahá'ís had things they would mix into food and drink to convert people. Tahmineh's parents had heard this and had refused to let her eat at our house.

She said to me, "I've always known it's a myth. I know that, but I didn't know what to do! My parents told me never to eat at your house. But, I love you. I love your parents. I don't want to hurt you."

"This just doesn't make sense!" I said. It seemed so unfair. I thought: Oh, her parents are so mean! Then, I said to my friend, "Tahmineh, you must not eat at our house. I won't offer you food at my home anymore. You've got to do what your parents say." That was a very important thing we were taught in Bahá'í Sunday School—always follow what your parents tell you. There was no question about disobeying her parents.

We were best friends—now closer than ever. I hoped we would get around this somehow, and we did. I told my parents about it, but I never said a word to her parents. I kept Tahmineh's secret with her family.

Then, do you know what we did? We started going to the neighborhood store together, because there we could buy things and eat them together on neutral ground. We enjoyed candies. We loved ice cream. Now, that was fun!

That was a difficult experience for a girl. Tahmineh and I were friends. We loved each other, yet she had heard this terrible thing about us from her parents and she carried that secret for a long time. Through the years, I have lost track of her; in 1960, my family moved to Germany and later, I moved to the United States and became a citizen. I'd love to find my friend again. I've Googled her and I keep looking for her on Facebook, but her name probably has changed through marriage.

I am hopeful about the future. We all are born to do something for the betterment of humanity. We need to share our stories, like this one, to help encourage a greater understanding of our diversity. If we just set our individual egos aside a little bit, we can see that truth.

Children understand it. I have seen the goodness in children myself. It melts my heart when I see friendships made, and kept, between different faiths. Sometimes that may mean sharing each other's secrets, but it is through friendship that we can see hope for our world.

CHAPTER 3

The Rev. Sandra Kay Gordon
A Surprise in a Hospital Room

Driving home—if I tell this story honestly—I didn't think I'd ever see her again.

The Rev. Sandra Gordon was an active Baptist all her life and felt a calling to the ordained ministry in the 1990s. Until her death in 2014, she served at the historic Greater New Mt. Moriah Missionary Baptist Church in Detroit. Her ministry was marked by a passion for bridging gaps between cultural communities, which she described as a legacy of her parents' approach to life and faith.

I CAN SEE now that I've been on a long journey of making connections between Judaism and Christianity, but it took an encounter with a young Jewish woman in a hospital room to turn up some of the stereotypes I had accumulated while growing up.

My family is Baptist, although we had known Jewish people through the years; my family had Jewish doctors while I was growing up, for example. But I really did not know much about Judaism when my first daughter was born in 1974. I had never had a Jewish friend.

That's why I was surprised on the day my daughter was born. From recovery, the hospital staff moved me to the room I would share during my stay at the hospital. The first thing I could see from the doorway was that I barely had a space in there! This other family had packed that room with flowers, balloons and lots of people. The other mother's name was Sarah, and the nurses actually had to ask her family to clear some space for me.

They were Jewish, and everybody in her whole extended family was making a big hoopla over her child.

Their affection and generosity and joy toward this baby were all very impressive to me, but I have to admit—my reaction also reopened stereotypes I'd heard from my peers while growing up. The assumptions people passed around when I was growing up were old stereotypes—you know—like the one that Jews have a lot of money; that Caucasians, in general, didn't like us; and that Caucasians lived out in the suburbs because they didn't want relationships with us. I could see that this family cared a whole lot about Sarah and her baby. But just one look at all the stuff in that room—all the gifts and flowers—told me these people had money.

As a little girl, I had experienced racism firsthand. In 1959, my family traveled back to my father's hometown in South Carolina for a family funeral. I was absolutely shocked when I saw doors labeled for "Whites" and other doors labeled for us. Then, my cousins invited me to go to the movies, and I was horrified to find that we couldn't just walk up to the front doors—only White people could do that. We were just children, but we were forced to walk around into the alley where there was a door back there, labeled for us to use. I realize now how much that experience traumatized me. I do remember that I cried all the way home from South Carolina. How could the world be so hateful?

I did have one big advantage growing up, because in my home, these biases were never taught against any group of people. My father worked for Chevrolet and my mother's jobs included working for the Catholic Archdiocese of Detroit; my parents never taught negative things about Jewish or Caucasian people. They worked with people from other cultures. So, I had my parents' balance in my life as well.

Now, I have to admit that on that day, when I walked into the hospital room with Sarah and her family filling the whole place—yes, I was a little jealous of Sarah.

I was a first-time mother, too. She had this whole garden sprouting over on her side of the room; I had one little, bitty flower someone had given me. With all of the gifts she had over there, on her side of the room, it was obvious they were rich. I got a few things, but nothing like that pile over on her side.

Now—truth be told—her baby was the very first grandchild on both sides of the family, so it was a very special event. In my family, mine wasn't the first grandchild—so, that was one big difference.

These events all took place back in the day, when mothers stayed in the hospital for a while and, as I recall, both Sarah and I had longer stays because of some complications. So we knew we'd be living side-by-side in that room for a while.

There was a curtain between the two beds, but we decided not to pull it—and, I'm so glad we didn't close that curtain! Instead, we began to talk. When all the visitors left, we were just two young mothers, talking about our lives and families and hopes for the future. We were tired, of course, but we sat up talking until the wee hours of the morning. She was so down-to-Earth, so pleasant, so kind. She became a good friend that first night.

But, I will tell you, there came a time when she left—a day or two before I did—and you know how, after something like that, people always say, "Oh, we'll be sure to get together!" Well, we did—and she actually did invite me to her house.

I debated whether to go. Did she really want me to come? Would I be comfortable? Would I know all the right things to do in her home? But I am an extroverted person, and I went out there, even though I was nervous. It turned out to be just great! She served lunch, and we put our babies down on the floor together. We talked and talked. When it was over, I said what you would expect: "Now, you'll have to come to my house."

Driving home—if I tell this story honestly—I didn't think I'd ever see her again. It was one thing for me to drive out to her house, but she had to come into Detroit to visit mine. It was one thing for us to visit just once, like we'd promised when she left the hospital. But to continue this as a real friendship? No, I didn't think it would happen.

Again, she surprised me. She really did want to come to my house. She had no problem coming into Detroit. She visited, and I served *her* lunch this time. Our babies played on the floor together and, once again, we talked and talked.

That friendship continued for a couple of years. I've lost track of her now, as sometimes happens with friends as years go by— but she was an important friend in my life.

What about all those old biases I had learned while growing up? They faded away. Now, I realize that I've always been on a pathway connecting my Christianity with the traditions of our Jewish neighbors. Now, I'm the assistant to the pastor at a nationally known church in Detroit: Greater New Mount Moriah. Our senior pastor—the Rev. Kenneth J. Flowers, is well-known for his work linking Christians and Jews. In 2008, I visited Israel and learned even more about how our faiths and histories connect in so many ways.

I'd like Sarah to know that our friendship was an important part of my own journey, from all that I saw in childhood—some of it quite traumatic—to the calling that I have today to spread the word about all the ways that Christians and Jews, together, can strengthen each other's lives.

Chapter 4

Ayesha Khan
Daring to Knock on a Door

Within the span of one year, I had gone from being a carefree, single student to a married woman and the mother of a baby girl.

Becoming a parent is a milestone in life that can suddenly connect us with complete strangers. Even if we share nothing else about our faith and culture with our neighbors, as new parents, we encounter a host of crises and questions that other parents have experienced before us. That's the connection Ayesha Khan discovered as a young mother in a suburban apartment complex in Southern California.

WHEN I WAS 19 years old, I emigrated from India to the United States with my family. After arriving in Chicago, my parents, sisters and I moved into a small two-bedroom apartment in the same building as my grandparents and uncles. I had always heard stories of what America was like, envisioning scenes from my favorite American books, movies and TV shows. However, the life I experienced in Chicago turned out to be quite different than what I had envisioned. America was not as glamorous as it had seemed on TV and films. Nonetheless, I was happy to be surrounded by my family and excitedly enrolled in a university in the Chicago area.

Two years later, at the age of 21, I married a man who my parents knew through mutual friends. Soon after my wedding, I once again packed all of my belongings and relocated thousands of miles from my family. My husband, Salman, was a mechanical engineer for an aerospace company near Los Angeles, California. Shortly after that, I became pregnant.

My husband and I had only one car and there wasn't any public transportation in the suburb where we lived. It was difficult for me to get around the area, so I spent most of my time alone in my apartment. Because I was new, I knew very few people living in the area. I found myself overwhelmed with all of the sudden changes in my life. Within the span of one year, I had gone from being a carefree, single student to a married woman and the mother of a baby girl.

The birth of our daughter, Aminah, filled the void I felt after leaving behind so much of my family in Chicago. I soon found myself swept up into the busy life of a mother caring for a young infant. My life revolved around my daughter, as I seemed to be constantly feeding her, changing her diapers and soothing her when she cried.

When Aminah was born, my mother came from Chicago to help me out with the baby. However, as soon as she left, I was overcome with the fear of spending time alone with the baby during the day while my husband was at work. After all, I was only 22 years old and felt inexperienced as a parent. My "baby blues" rapidly developed into the full range of anxiety and loneliness of postpartum depression, eclipsing my initial excitement as a young mother. More than ever, I missed my parents, sisters and the rest of my extended family in Chicago. Every day when my husband left for work, I would cry. The hours would pass so slowly as I waited for him to come home again. He didn't know what to make of my sudden change of behavior and would try his best to cheer me up. He would encourage us to go the park or a restaurant or a shopping mall as a family. But, no matter what he did, I felt my anxiety growing every day that I was left alone with my baby.

At the time, Salman and I lived in an apartment complex close to his work. It was right across from California State University and most of the tenants living in our building were students. The apartment directly across from ours was occupied by a woman in her early 80s—someone from a completely different generation and cultural background. My interactions with her had been limited to a brief exchange of greetings whenever our paths crossed in the building or parking lot. She introduced herself as Thelma Libby, but said I could call her Libby.

I was curious about my elderly neighbor. But, I remembered my close friends in Chicago telling me that American neighbors are reserved and like to keep to themselves. I was told: "It's not like back in India where everyone naturally interacts." That made sense to me, because in India neighbors often visit each other without formalities and share food. I saw little sign of that in America, so I took my friends' advice to heart. Better not disturb Libby!

One day, however, I felt so overwhelmed and desperate that I knocked on Libby's door and told her I needed some help with my baby for a few minutes. Libby instantly followed me back to my apartment and, although she was still a stranger to me, I felt at ease as I handed her my baby and climbed into the shower. The few minutes I had in the shower were enough to calm me down and I felt considerably better. I found that Libby's presence in my apartment gave me a sense of comfort and my anxiety immediately subsided.

I offered her tea and, for the first time, Libby and I chatted and got to know one another. Like me, she had recently moved to California. She and her husband had lived in Ohio until his death, when she decided to head west and relocate close to her daughter. She also felt lonely in her apartment, missing her husband and her friends in Ohio. Before I realized it, two hours had passed and the two of us had bonded. My daughter had fallen asleep in Libby's arms and Libby told me that it was the best feeling she'd had in a very long time. I thanked my kind neighbor profusely for helping me out. She said I could come to her place any time and to call her whenever I needed help. After Libby left, I realized that knocking on her door was one of the best decisions I had made.

After that, Libby and I saw each other frequently. Whenever I needed help or felt lonely I would either go to Libby's apartment or invite her over to my place. I looked forward to her lemonade and she enjoyed my Indian tea. The tenants of our apartment complex got used to seeing a young Indian mother with an infant out walking or sitting by the pool with this elderly lady. Libby said spending time with us made her so happy that she didn't dwell on her own isolation. I told Libby stories about Indian culture and showed her my Indian outfits and the array of Indian spices that my mom gave me. Libby taught me how to make American desserts like apple pie and chocolate chip cookies. She even wrote down the recipes for me on index cards, which I still have in my recipe box. Also, it was Libby who helped me with menu planning when had to I host the Thanksgiving dinner for the very first time and gave me important tips for cooking the perfect turkey.

Libby had never met a Muslim before, so I often talked to her about my faith traditions. She was fascinated watching me pray in my apartment and would ask me questions about the prayers and why I wore a hijab over my hair when I went outside. In exchange, Libby would tell me stories of her family in Ohio and the wonderful years she'd had with her husband. We bonded over our common relationships with family, friends, culture, traditions and basic humanity.

As I got to know Libby and felt more confident as a mother, my baby blues subsided and I started to feel more like my normal self. I stopped crying so much and no longer greeted my husband at the end of the day with swollen eyes. I enjoyed spending quality time with our daughter and had the comfort of knowing that my new friend was just next door if I ever needed her. My friendship with Libby made me realize that I had been wrong to assume she might not welcome my company simply because we seemed so different on the surface. In fact, it didn't matter that I was an Indian Muslim and she was a white Christian. We had a great friendship now.

I kept in contact with Libby after I moved from that apartment. She came to my new apartment when my second daughter, Saliha, was born, and brought her a beautiful baby blanket. Later that year, my husband got a new job and we moved from California to Michigan. A year later we were blessed with our son, Ridwan, and I became busy with three little ones.

After my move to Michigan I lost touch with Libby, but my friendship with her inspired me to reach out to people who are different from me and not to make assumptions about them. My friendship with Libby was instrumental in my decision to become involved in interfaith work, become a part of WISDOM's board, and to encourage others to create relationships that cross religious and cultural barriers that can seem more daunting than they really are.

CHAPTER 5

Shama Mehta
A Bollywood Song From Home

*What would my friends back home
think about this new friend?*

Like Ayesha Khan, Shama Mehta serves on the WISDOM board and has a passionate commitment to helping people make cross-cultural connections— because she discovered the importance of bridging those gaps at an early age. Shama also enjoys talking about her experiences as a lifelong Hindu as part of interfaith programs,

especially WISDOM's popular Five Women, Five Journeys program. Professionally, Shama is a Board Certified Chaplain with a Master's degree in Pastoral Ministry practicing as part of the spiritual care team at a major health system in Michigan.

ON A FRIGID January morning in Toronto, I was getting ready for my first day as a 12th-grade student in my first week living in Canada. The year was 2001 and I had just moved with my family from India.

Of course, before we had moved to our new home, I had heard stories about Toronto's religious, cultural and racial diversity—and I welcomed that. Before we made this long journey, I had been used to interacting with people from different faith traditions. India is a religiously diverse nation. But, I still was anxious. What was new to me in Canada was interacting with people from other races and nationalities.

This had not been an easy first week on my new continent. I had left behind everything I had ever known, and for a 16-year-old, the hardest part was leaving friends behind. To make things worse, my Indian hometown, Ahmedabad, was hit with a major earthquake less than 24 hours after we flew out of the airport.

I am a practicing Hindu and have always been involved in the way my family practices our faith. My family is also very open-minded. Growing up in India, I went to a school run by Seventh-day Adventists and had Hindu, Muslim, Christian, Jain and Sikh friends. Our school was located right next to a Jewish-run school. We also had a close family member who married into a Muslim family and thus my social and personal interactions were all religiously diverse.

As I walked towards school, the temperature was more than 10 degrees below zero Fahrenheit—a stark contrast to growing up in a city where temperatures often topped 100 degrees! I began to think about all my friends who were no longer with me. How were their families faring after the earthquake? This was some years before we all used social media on our smartphones. I was cut off. I did not know anyone—not one person. As I worried about how I would ever make friends in this new high school, tears began to well up in my eyes. A series of embarrassing first-day crises did not improve my mood: I couldn't work the combination on my locker! I walked into the wrong classroom!

Finally, I reached the door of my first class. As I waited, other kids gathered around me, but made no effort to talk to me.

Then, a girl appeared in front of me with long hair worn in a perfect braid—singing a Bollywood song! I had to smile, even before she energetically said, "Hi!! Are you new?"

Relieved that someone bothered to talk to me, I said right away, "Yes, I am Shama. I just came from India last week. Today is my first day."

That was all my new friend needed to hear. She said, "I am Hina. Welcome to Boylen!"

She told me that her family moved to Toronto when she was in middle school—from their home in Pakistan. Now, I was hesitant. Could I befriend someone from Pakistan? Ever since the partition with India in the 1940s, there have been tensions between the two nations. In 2001, memories of recent conflicts were fresh in both of our minds. I had a strong feeling of patriotism toward India, especially because I was a newly arrived immigrant.

I thought: *How would my friends back in India react if they knew my first-ever friend in Canada is a Pakistani?* Our different faiths were not a problem. Both of us had experienced religious diversity. What I had never experienced was a Pakistani friend.

However, this clearly was not the issue for my friend. She understood the conflicts between the two nations, but her years of experience in Toronto already had changed her perspectives on a lot of things. My new friend took me under her wing on my very first day and, over lunch, introduced me to her group of friends: a Pakistani Muslim, a Bangladeshi Muslim, a Sri Lankan Hindu and a Vietnamese Buddhist. She made sure that I was included in their circle.

I learned a powerful lesson that day: what it means to go out of one's way to make someone feel welcome. From that day forward, I promised myself that I would reach out to every new student at the school so they would not feel that they were alone or isolated.

Our friendship continued to grow. Both of us matured spiritually and we enjoyed long conversations when Hina started wearing hijab over her hair. Hina supported my own vocation as a Hindu chaplain.

As I reflect upon those high school years, I am proud to say that this same group of friends continues to be my best friends today. Though some of us live in different cities now, we all continue to talk to each other through group texts and we actively share in each other's daily lives. My friendship with these amazing women continues to provide me with a solid foundation and belief that it is indeed possible to have friendships that bridge seemingly vast ethnic, national and religious differences.

CHAPTER 6

The Rev. Rose M. Cooper
The Enduring Importance of Presence

"You made it again!" She replied simply, *"This is what I do."*

The Rev. Rose Cooper is both an academic, serving as associate professor of communication at Oakland University, and a minister at Renaissance Unity in Michigan. In addition, she is a television producer and enjoys talking to groups about spirituality, communication and education. That wide range of interests provided the opening for an unusual friendship that began with intellectual curiosity and grew into something far deeper.

I MET NOHA at church.

That may seem unlikely because Noha is Muslim and I am Christian, part of the Unity movement that originated more than a century ago in the U.S. Given that we embrace diversity, it is not uncommon for me to meet someone from another faith at my church. People of various religious backgrounds sometimes visit, take or teach classes or attend services regularly. Going beyond church services or classes to share parts of the person's culture, though, was a new experience for me.

During my tenure as director of education at Renaissance Unity, Noha applied to teach her Imagination Unconscious Communication course (IUC). Reading her proposal, I was fascinated with the course content. Finally meeting her, I was also delighted by her loving spirit. As we talked, we realized that she shared my interest in modalities that enhance the well-being of the whole person—body, mind and spirit—and I shared her love of Middle Eastern food.

Noha and I began meeting periodically for lunch, alternating our choice of restaurants from her side of metropolitan Detroit to mine. One day, after lunch, we walked into a Middle Eastern grocery store so Noha could buy a few items and also familiarize me with various foods and products. She was quite the tour guide, pointing out the uses and benefits of various foods. Amazed at the large space and the variety of items stocked in this store, I looked around with interest—and wound up purchasing lentils, dates and chamomile tea.

On another lunch occasion, when meeting at the specified time and place became difficult, Noha said, "Come to my home. I will make something."

I arrived to find a beautiful tray of fruits, vegetables and pastries. The main treat, though, was two friends talking, undisturbed, for hours in the comfort of a home.

Noha's students and clients respected and appreciated her healing work. I learned that firsthand. Noha came to see my mother, who lived with me, and gave her a healing treatment. Later, when Noha planned a reception for her students and clients, she invited my mother and me to attend.

Upon arrival at Noha's home, I realized that the reception was on the lower level, which required descending and ascending a flight of stairs. Mama was ambulatory, but was used to handling only one or two stairs. I decided, simply, to give greetings and return home, but Noha encouraged us to try the stairs with her help.

"She can make it," she told me and then turned to my mother. "I will help you."

Step by step—with Noha in front and me behind my mother—we helped her move down the flight of 10 steps. After successfully arriving downstairs, Noha directed Mama to a comfortable armchair, elevated her feet and acted as the doting host. I thought of the old adage, "A friend in need is a friend indeed."

The Fourth of July is my holiday for hosting family and friends. Usually 30 to 40 people gather in my backyard: children playing on the swing set, slide and waterslide; older children playing volleyball; and adults sitting at picnic tables or in lawn chairs around the yard. This time, I invited Noha to join us. Noha came, brought a dessert and stayed for a while as my sisters and some other family members and friends greeted and talked with her. She was a true sport in a gathering that I imagine could have felt overwhelming.

The next year, Noha invited me to join her family and her brother's family one evening for *Iftar*, the meal to break the day's fast during Ramadan. I felt honored to share a meal during this holy time in her faith. Not sure what to expect upon arrival, I found the scene casual and comfortable. On the table was quite an array of Middle Eastern food: fattoush, lentil soup, rice, hummus, mujaddara, cookies, dates, along with a beef dish and a chicken dish. Seating was either at the table or on the comfortable sofa and chairs in the living room. Receiving kind greetings when introduced to Noha's family made me feel welcome. Although I talked mostly with Noha and her sister-in-law, Noha's sons also chatted a bit about college. The evening reminded me of exactly what it was: a family holiday meal.

What I have found most meaningful in this intercultural friendship is Noha's presence. This year I experienced two deaths in my immediate family—my mother's, which I had long anticipated, in February, and my brother's unexpectedly in May. Noha received the information each time in a text message, as did many other people. I had no clear idea who might attend the service. But when I walked out of the church after my mother's funeral, I saw Noha among the crowd waiting. She made her way over to me to offer condolences.

Similarly, when my brother's memorial service ended, before I exited the building, Noha came up to me to greet me and offer condolences. I said to her, "Noha, you made it again! This makes me feel so good."

She replied simply, "This is what I do."

Of course not everyone can be there for meaningful events. However, for those who can and those who will, their presence is a blessing. I am blessed to have met Noha. She is indeed my friend.

CHAPTER 7

Cheryl Zuhirah Ware El-Amin
'Working Hard' with Co-workers

It's so easy to misunderstand other people if you don't have an opportunity to talk honestly.

Cheryl was raised Presbyterian, then converted to Islam in 1976. Her lifelong pursuit of education led her to obtain a doctorate in 2009 in human services with a specialty in clinical social work. She is a school social worker and also is active in charitable and religious groups, including the mosque where her husband serves as an imam.

I AM A quiet person. I grew up as an only child, without a lot of other children running around our home, but I have always enjoyed meeting new people—especially people from other faiths and ethnic backgrounds. After my years of training in social work, I've learned not to be judgmental of others. When I meet people, I try to relate to them just as they are. I always assume that people have an essence of good within them, and I always try to relate to someone's best essence.

I have a longtime friend whom I met back in the late 1980s; I remember that she was the first Caucasian person with whom I developed a close friendship. We were both social workers at a hospital. When I was hired, I was assigned to share an office with her—and it was not a big office, so we got to know each other right away.

We shared several things: We both had a Presbyterian background; we both had grown up as an only child; and we both now had children of our own. We talked honestly as colleagues—and, as we got to know each other, we also talked just as girlfriends. We would joke sometimes as we found ourselves discussing people's assumptions about race and ethnicity.

We encountered some of those stereotypes we discussed right there at the hospital. She is about 10 years older than me, and I'm African-American. We shared a small office space. So, occasionally, when she was out of the office, I'd find people sticking their head in our doorway and giving me messages for her. It was obvious that they took one look at me and just assumed I was her secretary.

I didn't get angry at such things, but I did correct people. I'd say: "I am not her secretary. But I will tell her when I see her."

There are a lot of assumptions people carry around with them that are difficult to get rid of, because people often feel awkward talking about them. I remember one woman calling me on the telephone because she wanted to clear up a few things in her head about this "Black thing."

I remember she asked me, "Are you enraged?" She said, "I've heard that because of all the years of oppression in African-American history, there's this underlying anger." I guess she thought we all automatically shared this kind of free-floating anger and that we were all enraged. She called me with this question because she was concerned about a relationship with another African-American person. She thought she would double-check her assumptions about this "Black thing" with someone who might explain it to her honestly.

I explained that there's a lot of diversity among people. I do feel strongly about many things, but the idea that we all carry around the same free-floating feelings? Well, speaking for myself, I've never felt the kind of rage she described. I have been militant about some issues over the years that have mattered to me, but I don't carry a permanent rage. The real point here is that people are diverse.

I also discovered that I, myself, had assumptions about race. As my work continued at the hospital and I became better friends with this woman in the office, I began to realize that I had been making some assumptions about White people. I realized that there were far more Caucasian ethnicities and backgrounds than I had realized before. I had tended to mentally lump White people into one group without many distinctions, and my friend was happy to talk about this, especially when we'd encounter some new person. She might say: Oh, well, *this* person comes from a particular ethnic background and there are a lot of distinctive cultural issues here. Or, we might talk about social distinctions. She might say: Now, *that* person is what we'd call "old money," and people from that background tend to have *these* kinds of experiences.

I enjoyed our conversations. It's so easy to misunderstand other people if you don't have an opportunity to talk honestly.

We were good friends for a while, and then we went through years when we didn't see each other. I took a job in school social work and she moved to a different hospital. We kept in touch occasionally by email until one day, about a year ago, when she remembered that my husband enjoys golf and picked up the telephone to tell me about a golf tournament near her home. She had tickets to the tournament and thought my husband might enjoy seeing it. I stopped by her new hospital to pick up the tickets and, after that, our friendship picked up again.

Some time after that, my husband and I renewed our wedding vows after 31 years of marriage, and she came to that. It was wonderful. She got to see my children again, all grown up now.

As a Muslim woman, I know how many misperceptions there are about us. People assume that, since I cover my hair now, I'm forced to do that. And that's just not true. It's a choice I've made. I didn't always cover my hair; I choose to do that now. No one is forcing me.

Here's another example: People will say, "Oh, you're Muslim, so you don't believe in Jesus."

And I say, "What? That's not true. I believe in Jesus. I don't believe he was God, but Jesus is a very important part of Islam."

I've come to see that working on relationships with other people is a lifelong process. It really is. There's a verse in the Qur'an from Surah 94 that reads:

When thou art free (from thine immediate task), still labour hard, And to thy Lord turn (all) thy attention.

What it means is: You're never really finished with anything. When you're free from your immediate task, keep working hard, because there's still more to be done. The passage says "with every difficulty, there is relief." So, there is encouragement along the way, but we're not supposed to fall into contentment and inactivity. In our relationships, especially, we need to keep working. You never really "arrive" in life. You're always arriving— G'd willing.

Part III

Surprised by the Neighbors

We may assume that the community around us is hostile—until someone surprises us with the hopeful potential of friendship.

CHAPTER 8

Supreet Kaur Singh
Often, We Stand Alone

A lot of people I come across in daily life think I'm a Hindu. I tell them I'm a Sikh, and they say, 'Okay.' That doesn't mean anything to them.

The stories in this book are about friendship and Supreet, as a lifelong Sikh, has found important friendships through the interfaith women's group WISDOM. In Supreet's story, she conveys the  uncomfortable feeling of isolation that many people feel when they are part of smaller religious groups. This is especially poignant for Sikhs because their sacred traditions require them to dress in ways that make them visual targets whenever they travel in America.

I GREW UP in India, and at that time, I had friends who were Hindu, Christian and Muslim. I was brought up around people of different backgrounds and different religions.

But in India, Sikhs are a minority. And, often, minorities aren't considered as important as the majority. People would make jokes about Sikhs—would make fun of us—and we couldn't do much or say much because we were the minority.

Later, we lived through a few years when attacks were made on Sikhs. In 1984, Indira Gandhi, the Prime Minister of India, was attacked and murdered by some people who were Sikhs. After that, there was turbulence throughout India and a lot of innocent Sikhs were killed. The Sikhs were not prepared for these brutal attacks. Many died. *The Widow Colony: India's Unsettled Settlement* is a 2006 documentary film that shows what happened in 1984 and afterward.

We Sikhs need to tell the story of our faith more widely. Most people have heard the word "Sikh" and know that it is the name of a person of our faith, but they don't know more than that. Most people don't know the significance of men wearing a turban (a turban is supposed to give the look of a saint, or of a holy person). They don't know that we believe in eating *jhatka* meat, meat from an animal that was killed in our traditional way with no pain.

The word "*jhatka*" is like the word Jewish people use for properly prepared food: kosher. Or Muslims say: halal. Everyone has an idea what it means when he or she hears someone use the word "kosher." But, when I am at a restaurant, it is hard to find someone to ask about whether any of the meat is *jhatka*. No one even knows the word, in most cases. Our process of preparing the meat follows principles similar to kosher or halal preparation—but our traditions are different and the process is different. Imagine the difficulty we face at restaurants, if we want to eat meat. Of course, some Sikhs don't eat meat at all.

Living in a minority community is difficult enough, but the media add to the problem by portraying Sikhs on TV and in movies in stereotypical roles. Sikh men and women have few opportunities in the entertainment business, so it becomes easier for people who write and produce TV shows and movies to feel they can make fun of Sikhs.

I have lived with this difficult challenge all my life. Now, when my sons go to a mall, they get noticed, too. We do try to explain who we are, if people ask, but many people don't really want to learn much.

A lot of people I come across in daily life think I'm a Hindu. I tell them I'm a Sikh, and they say, "Okay." That doesn't mean anything to them.

Now, I do have some American friends who are not Sikhs. We Sikhs believe in hospitality and welcoming people who are not a part of our faith. We welcome people to visit our *gurdwaras*, our houses of worship. Anyone can go, not just Sikhs. The WISDOM women understand this. In WISDOM, we welcome everyone of every faith, too. We talk about the meaning of our beliefs and traditions.

I am hopeful that people will want to learn more and will want to make friends from other faiths—if we give them opportunities like this. In my own life, I find that if someone is willing to tell me about their religion, I think it is amazing.

I think others will find all of the world's different faiths amazing, too.

CHAPTER 9

Elaine Greenberg
Holidays and Huffy Neighbors

You can imagine the altercation that followed! It ended with our neighbor walking out of our house in a huff, mumbling something about "Jews."

Elaine Greenberg is a musician, a cancer survivor and an active member of her Jewish community. For many years, she led choirs and taught music—and now she uses her own vocal talents to help cancer patients and their caregivers.

WHEN I WAS a young girl, Hanukkah was not a big holi-day, and gift-giving was not what it is today, so our family—my uncles, aunts, grandmother—put our names in a container, and everyone picked out one name and that was the person they were to buy a gift for. My Uncle Hy had my name one year and bought the complete score (on 78 records) of Walt Disney's *Snow White and The Seven Dwarfs*. I still have that album. When my chil-dren were small, my family still wasn't making a big deal about Hanukah, but one year we decided to give the children eight gifts—one for each night of the holiday. I tried to be very clever, and on the last night, each one of our children—ages 4 to 10 (well, maybe not the 4-year-old)—got a key to the house. They thought that was fabulous! How times have changed!

But my favorite story of all is from the earlier years of my life.

This goes all the way back to 1944, when I was just about to turn 9 years old and my mother and father finally saved enough money to buy us our very own home. Such excitement! The house was everything my parents could have asked for, with the exception of the outer color of the house, which was dark red, almost brown, and the ceiling in the kitchen, which was a blinding, bright red.

We had a fireplace, although it wasn't lit too terribly often. To my father's delight, we even had a screened-in porch that ran the entire width of the house. My father spent many a hot summer night sleeping on that porch and, since there was no such thing as air conditioning, we all spent many summer days and nights on that front porch.

In the corner of the kitchen, there was a small shelf about chest-high that served as a telephone shelf. On the white walls surrounding that telephone shelf were a ton of telephone num-bers. You see, my father would call Information (no charge in those days) and didn't have paper readily available, so he wrote the numbers on the kitchen walls. I do believe, when we sold that house, the numbers were still on the walls.

On one side of this house, we had what was called a four-flat where four separate families lived. But on the other side of our house, there was a single-family dwelling that was somewhat smaller than ours. The husband and wife who lived there were Frank and Marie Honel.

Unfortunately, our first encounter with the Honels was not a pleasant one. It involved a lamp that had come with our new home—one of those things the previous owners had left behind.

When Mrs. Honel paid us her very first visit, we found out that she and her husband had come from Germany in 1938. When we moved into our home in 1944, the war was still going on in Europe, so here we had a Jewish family and a German family living next door to each other. In itself, this could have caused problems.

But the lamp touched off the conflict. Mrs. Honel came to visit us because she insisted that the previous owners were aware of her affection for this particular lamp—and had promised that it would be given to her in the transition. When the lamp never made it to Mrs. Honel's house, she apparently decided she would come over and claim it from the home's new occupants. My mother knew nothing about this supposed arrangement. In fact, she rather liked that lamp.

You can imagine the altercation that followed! It ended with our neighbor walking out of our house in a huff, mumbling something about "Jews." We didn't speak to them for quite a while. I don't know how long.

But, eventually, a kind of peace settled in between the two families.

When our neighbors emigrated from Germany, they brought with them a household full of furniture. Their house was cozy and comfortable with antiques and all kinds of other interesting stuff they brought with them from their homeland.

Among their belongings were beautiful Christmas decorations, including heirloom tree ornaments that they used every year.

Mr. and Mrs. Honel had no children. As I recall it, Mrs. Honel seemed almost reluctant one winter when she surprised me by asking if I would like to trim their Christmas tree with them. Their ornaments were beautiful, and I wanted to help.

I had to ask for my parents' permission, of course. They were Orthodox Jews, but my mother still gave her permission. And we hit it off! From then on, the Honel tree wasn't trimmed until "their girl"—and that was me—was there to help them.

How well I remember those figures under their tree that depicted the birth of Jesus.

Of course, I didn't know that one day I would visit Israel and, as part of my trip, I would visit Bethlehem and see where Jesus was born.

We even exchanged gifts. The Honels got Christmas gifts from us. We got Hanukah gifts from them.

I treasure those memories of sitting in their home, a young girl sharing with this elderly couple. In their wonderful kitchen, I would talk with Mrs. Honel as I helped her bake goodies in an old-fashioned wood-burning stove.

Why do I cherish this memory?

Because of the love I felt in that connection with the Honels— and the forgiveness that allowed us finally to cross over all that had separated us and finally share that love.

CHAPTER 10

Bobbie Lewis
Miss Loreaux's Hanukkah Menorah

I felt uneasy. What had I said that was funny?

Millions of children first experience the diversity of the larger community in public school classrooms—so teachers can play a transformative role in their lives. Throughout Bobbie Lewis's long career as a writer, editor and communication specialist, she immersed herself in the diverse community of metropolitan Detroit. Although semi-retired now, she remains active in many groups, including on WISDOM's board, and continues to write for the *Detroit Jewish News*. Her adult confidence in welcoming diverse friends and colleagues was encouraged very early in her life.

IT WAS THE beginning of Hanukkah, the eight-day festival that commemorates the victory of the Jews in the 2nd century BCE over the Assyrian Greeks who had invaded their country.

My family was not at all observant, but we always lit candles in the eight-branched menorah—one on the first day, two on the second, and so on until all eight (plus a "servant" candle used to light the others) were ablaze on the last night.

I was 6, and the only Jewish girl in the first grade at Kennedy Crossan Elementary School in northeast Philadelphia. We lived in a very Jewish neighborhood of houses newly built in the early 1950s. But my street was near the border of that new neighborhood and a much older, heavily German-American community. Our house stood within the boundaries of the older neighborhood's school.

My mother had a miniature Hanukkah menorah that held birthday candles, and she let me take it to school for show and tell. I gave my garbled version of the reason for the holiday: There was a nasty king who invaded ancient Israel and took over the holy Temple, destroying everything in it. The Jews fought back and retook the Temple. But when they went to light the lamp that had to be kept burning at all times, they found only enough oil to last one day. They lit the lamp and it stayed lit for eight days, until they could get more oil. I told my classmates how we light candles in the menorah every night for eight nights to remember this miracle.

The other students had never heard of Hanukkah. Most of them had probably never met a Jew, and they certainly didn't know anything about Jewish practices. Some of them started tittering.

I felt uneasy. What had I said that was funny?

That's when my teacher, Miss Loreaux, showed her mettle.

Emily Loreaux was a tall, older woman with tight, gray curls and a kind face. Few students could spell her name. Many couldn't even pronounce it, calling her "Miss Low Row." She had been at Crossan a long time and would be there for many years to come.

We didn't know anything about her private life, but occasionally we'd see her walking away from school, wearing a long, green, wool coat and a little, brown, close-fitting hat, in the company of a man. We students speculated, spinning all kinds of scenarios—but we never knew her real story. Years later, when my younger sister was still at Crossan, Miss Loreaux married and became Mrs. Murdock.

That day at the start of Hanukkah, as I stood uncomfortably in front of the class with my birthday-candle menorah, the giggling rose. That is, until Miss Loreaux stared down those giggling students. She said, "I'm lighting my menorah tonight."

The class quieted immediately. A few students threw admiring glances my way. I couldn't contain my excitement. As soon as school let out, I ran home and told my mother, "Guess what? Miss Loreaux is Jewish! She said she's going to light her Hanukkah menorah tonight!"

My mother smiled quietly. She explained to me that Miss Loreaux was not Jewish but that she was a "*mensch*"—an upright, honorable, decent person. She made me understand what a nice thing she had done, identifying herself with me so that I wouldn't feel like an outsider.

I can't say I never felt like an outsider at that school. My friends got Christmas presents and Easter baskets, went to Sunday school and sang in their church choirs. I did not. I ate gefilte fish, kugel and bagels with lox and cream cheese. They did not. Their grandparents were "American" and spoke like normal people. My grandparents were born in Europe and spoke with heavy accents. But throughout my seven years at Kennedy Crossan Elementary School, I never heard an anti-Semitic remark. No one ever made fun of me or denigrated me because of my religion, and no one excluded me from any activities because I wasn't "like them."

I also learned a lot about mainline Christianity, including some beautiful hymns and Bible readings that were part of every assembly in those days before the Supreme Court declared them to be state-sanctioned prayer and no longer permitted in our schools. I agreed with the ruling, but was also happy that I'd had that exposure.

Most of all, I learned that a good teacher imparts more than the three Rs, and Miss Loreaux was one of the best.

CHAPTER 11

Parwin Anwar
A Harrowing Escape Inspires a Life of Compassionate Service

This is not right! I was determined to change this situation for this little girl.

The challenges of building new relationships are greater for refugees, many of whom arrive with fears stemming from the trauma they have survived. Parwin Anwar was born in Kabul, Afghanistan, and survived a harrowing escape from her war-torn homeland, followed by a difficult transition into the American workforce. Ultimately, she decided to use her own experiences to help students from immigrant families in the Macomb Intermediate School District northeast of Detroit. Her knowledge of Farsi, Pashto, Urdu and Arabic equipped her for service as a bilingual tutor. Her strength and her faith have led her to become a force of compassion in her community.

IN THE HEAT of July 1984, my husband, Qadir, and I had to leave our homeland of Afghanistan. This was in the middle of the Soviet-Afghan War, during a time of increasing resistance against the Soviet-backed government. At least 1 million civilians lost their lives during that decade-long conflict. The situation was so dangerous that my parents and siblings had left the country earlier. By 1984, Qadir and I feared for the safety of our own young family. Soldiers would storm into homes in our community without any warning and seize people. Some of my friends were taken—and were never seen again. There were explosions in buses, theaters and other public places. Our son was 5, our daughter was 3 and I was six months pregnant. Qadir and I decided we had to flee.

When we left our home, like so many refugees around the world, we could only carry a few things with us. We could not reveal to anyone that we were trying to leave the country, so we were unable to say proper farewells. Instead, we told my husband's family that we were just going to visit a relative for a couple of days. Then, all too soon, we were traveling beyond any of our familiar surroundings. My heart was heavy, my tears fell but, at that time, I did not dare to speak to anyone else about my sorrow. At the start, our journey began with a short ride in a truck, but then we were on foot for the next 150 miles. My fears grew hour by hour, day by day! *How would I survive this dangerous trek as a pregnant woman trying to keep up with the others while my husband and I struggled to tend to our young son and daughter?*

No one in our group had good walking shoes. In keeping with our cover story, we all wore traditional clothing, complete with bangle bracelets and henna for the women. In case we were stopped at a checkpoint, our story was that we were going to a nearby village to attend a wedding. We had a horse and two donkeys, which we used to carry our group's meager provisions. When we started, we carried some food with us, but all too soon the heat spoiled everything. We used up our water quickly, too. Whenever we came to a river, we drank and filled up every bottle we could. Sometimes villagers gave us food and water, but most days we had very little.

Because I was pregnant, I sometimes rode the horse, but that proved to be dangerous. While trying to get down from the horse, my dress caught in the saddle. I fell and was scraped the length of my torso. Mainly, I walked—all day long in the searing summer heat.

Then, there was the Soviet bombardment. At that time, Soviet forces attacked groups of people like our cluster of refugees. We quickly learned that any place we spent the night would be bombarded the next day. There was one time when we had to hide in a valley for eight hours until the attacks stopped.

One night, in a pitch-dark stretch of desert, we heard a loud order for us to stop. We all froze on the spot, blind to whatever lay ahead of us. I was on the horse at that point, and sat nervously, trying to peer into the darkness. Suddenly, a red bolt of light sped toward me! Even as that bolt appeared, I screamed and fell from the horse. This time, my husband caught me before I hit the ground. I was dazed. Somehow, we survived that encounter and wound up at a safe resting place. I was in so much pain that I could not straighten my body. I could not move. I prayed that I could take just one step and managed painfully to do that. I was crying and praying and trying to move. The other refugees agreed to delay our departure the next day until noon, due to my pain.

At one point in our journey, I felt that I could not continue. I feared that I might have my baby at any moment. I feared I would collapse. That's when my 5-year-old son volunteered to walk behind me promising to catch me if I fell. That loving and courageous encouragement—and constant prayer—kept me going.

Eventually, we came to a tall mountain with no road around it. We had to crawl up this rocky slope—so shear and harsh that some members of our group lost toenails in the climb. Even faced with this obstacle, my children and my husband and I kept going. That is the power of love and faith and prayer.

After five days, our small refugee group arrived in Pakistan. My daughter was born there in Pakistan. After eight months, we were granted refugee status and came to the United States. As we settled into our Michigan home, my husband and I had a fourth child, a son.

As I look back at the early part of my life, I recall a happy and comfortable family before the Soviet conflict. My mother worked as a teacher; my father served as minister of commerce. Our family encouraged education and community service. I am a university graduate. In Kabul, I taught Pashto language classes in a high school. Qadir worked in a bank. Then, our entire world was torn apart by the conflict and we almost lost our lives trying to reach freedom on that 150-mile odyssey to Pakistan.

The trauma that refugees experience stays with us throughout our lives. I found great peace of mind as our family settled into the United States—but, all these years later, I still don't like the sound of thunder or the sound of fireworks. The sound of a helicopter automatically takes me back to the war zone.

Before my children began school, I stayed at home with them. Finding work is always a challenge for refugees. As I began looking for work, I even took a grueling job at a gas station for a while. Always, I remembered my father's advice: "As long as you work with honesty and dignity, no job is bad." In Kabul, I had started my career as an educator, so I was drawn to the schools. To become a teacher here, however, I would have had to upgrade my teaching credentials. So, I applied for other work within the school system. Finally, I got a call from the bilingual education department of Macomb County, which coordinates educational programs for suburbs north of Detroit. They were looking for someone who could speak Pashto, Farsi and Urdu—and they wanted me to start right away. I was thrilled!

That's how my 25 years with MISD began, starting as a bilingual tutor helping kids from Afghanistan, India and Pakistan primarily. I considered it a perfect job. My schedule now matched our children's school schedule. I became committed to helping these children build new relationships and succeed in their classes.

My advocacy expanded. One year during Ramadan, I befriended a young fifth-grade student who was fasting, surrounded by all the delicious smells in the cafeteria and hundreds of other children eagerly enjoying the food. I suggested that she sit in the library and read, instead of sitting in the cafeteria. But, I was stunned to learn from the school staff that this was not possible. Young children, even if they were fasting, were not allowed to go somewhere else during the lunch period.

I thought: *This is not right!* I was determined to change this situation for this little girl—and all the other children who might be facing this situation during Ramadan. As I worked on that policy change, my reputation spread as a cross-cultural advocate. I was asked to speak at the annual conference of the Michigan Association of Bilingual Education, specifically to talk about Muslims and Ramadan. That talk went well and soon I was providing cultural-awareness education for teachers. I helped to showcase Afghanistan at an annual international event hosted by Macomb schools. Awareness of the compassionate approach I took to this cross-cultural work spread further and my own confidence increased. Eventually, my appearances on behalf of these issues ranged from regional television stations to talks and conferences in other cities outside Macomb County. Whenever I lift my voice, I try to share the richness of our cultures and religions—and to convey our life experiences so that educators and parents can help all of the students in the community thrive in our multicultural society. As I prepare my talks, I think frequently about this passage from the Qur'an:

> O mankind! We created you from a single pair of a Male and a Female, and made you into nations and tribes, that you may know each other—and not despise each other.

As the Qur'an says, the more we learn about each other as humans, the more we learn to love and accept one another of all faiths and nationalities.

CHAPTER 12

Gigi Salka
The Hardest Thing I've Ever Had to Do

I was nervous. Anxious. Worried. All of the above! People don't know how to react when you make a change like this.

Gigi is Muslim and a mother of three children living in Bloomfield Hills. She is an active volunteer in her community.

THE HARDEST THING I've ever had to do in my life was to walk into my child's school for the first time after I began wearing the headscarf that is distinctive for Muslim women. My son was in fifth grade at the time.

This all happened in February 2003. My husband and I finally decided to perform the pilgrimage, the Hajj. We had wanted to make the Hajj for years but, each time, something would come up. There always seemed to be so many reasons why we shouldn't go. The kids were too young. My husband couldn't leave work. It was a very serious decision. As Muslims we like to say that, when you go on the Hajj, you come back home the way you were born. It's like all your sins are erased and you're opening a new book in your life. For me, I knew that meant I would start wearing the headscarf.

I had not been wearing the headscarf and, because I hadn't worn it, I didn't stick out so obviously as Muslim in public. Just look at me and my kids—white, blond hair—we kind of blend into the American environment. But the question of wearing the headscarf had been weighing on my shoulders for some time. I grew up in America, attended university, had a successful career, married a loving husband and began raising my family. God has blessed me with so much. I wanted to start wearing the headscarf regularly as a sign of my faith, but I didn't have the strength.

It wasn't a big struggle for me to decide whether I should wear it. I wanted to wear it. I had already begun to change how I dressed. I only wore long skirts or pants and long-sleeve shirts. It is all about being modest; in dress, in attitude and in self-presentation. In my opinion, the headscarf was just another step toward greater modesty, but I could not garner the strength to put it on and wear it regularly. The biggest problem for me was the idea of facing people I had known for a long time—now, wearing the headscarf. That's hard for many American Muslim women, I think. I know it was for me.

When we went on the Hajj, though, I knew that I'd definitely want to start covering my hair.

As the Hajj season nears each year, the excitement in the Muslim community grows. People start talking about who is going on the Hajj this year, and how they are preparing for this once-in-a-lifetime trip. Every year I remained at home, yearning to join the pilgrims, but this year was different: There were so many friends planning their trip that it was impossible to stay away. Although in retrospect it was probably the most inopportune time, my husband and I decided at the last minute to perform the Hajj that year. We were so late in deciding that we wound up Federal Expressing our passports, and we didn't get our travel documents until we got to the airport. We were hurrying around and weren't even sure that we'd be able to make the flight, but finally, we did get on the plane. This was a rushed trip, but I felt a sense of inner peace and security that I had never felt before. God gave me patience.

As we were hurrying around and getting ready to go, a Muslim friend came to visit and say goodbye. When I saw her, I suddenly had all these questions. I asked, "When am I going to put my headscarf on? The imam is coming with us on the plane, so should I put it on before I get on the plane? Should I put it on over there in Saudi Arabia? Or, when I'm coming home? How do I wear it right?"

So many questions!

She said: "Just put it on! Get it over with!"

So, I put it on as we went to the airport. Women wear the headscarf throughout the entire Hajj in Saudi Arabia. Then, when we were coming home on the plane, once again there were all these questions! I kept asking my husband: "Do I keep it on? Do I wear it when I get off the plane? What am I going to do?"

He was of no help. "It is your decision," was the answer he repeated over and over again.

I got home and basically stayed at home for a week. I kept worrying: What do I do? I can't take it off and, if I go out wearing it, what will people think when they see me for the first time?

Then, soon, I had to face going into my children's school. I'm very active there. I couldn't stay away. There was a parent meeting I had to attend. Coming back from the Hajj, I did feel spiritually rejuvenated and stronger as a Muslim, but on that first day walking toward the school, I couldn't stop asking myself: How will people react?

I hadn't planned anything that I might say to people. If they asked questions, I would try to answer them. That's how I am. But I really didn't know what I would say to explain it all as I drove up that day. Our school is designed so there's a parking lot and then there's a *loooong* sidewalk that leads up to the school. There's no way around it. You have to park and walk up this *loooong* sidewalk.

I parked my minivan and I made that walk very *sloooowly.*

No one at the school knew I had gone on Hajj or that I would start wearing this scarf. And on that first day I went to the school, I knew that my son's teacher had gone on maternity leave while we were away, so I didn't know the new teacher at all. I was nervous.

Anxious.

Worried.

All of the above!

People don't know how to react when you make a change like this, so it puts more of a burden on you to break the ice. They wonder: Am I supposed to say something? Or not say something? Respond to this change? Or ask something? Or is it offensive to ask questions?

Finally, I reached the door. I walked into the school and, as soon as you walk in there's this media center where people congregate for meetings. As usual, people were gathered there.

I saw a friend and I walked right toward her. And she said: "Oh, Gigi! You've covered your hair!"

I didn't know what to say. I just said: "Yeah."

She surprised me. She asked, "Are you making a political statement?"

I didn't expect that question! I was still so nervous. I answered very slowly: "Nooooo. No, I'm not." That thought never even crossed my mind, I was only trying in my humble way to fulfill a spiritual desire that I had worked so hard to attain.

I suddenly realized: They're looking at me and they're wondering why I've just made this change. This was when the memory of 9/11 was still fresh in everyone's mind. So many things ran through my mind. Then, I just began to talk to my friend. I described the Hajj and what it meant to me. I explained to her how it was a spiritual rejuvenation and how I felt so much closer to my Creator during this time. I explained how I felt a sense of calm, peace and happiness upon my return. She listened.

We were friends—so she listened. And we remained good friends after that, because she was open. I remember that: She listened to my story.My life has changed since I began to wear the headscarf. Life does get a little bit harder when you decide to do this. You do have to keep wondering: Am I representing my faith properly? I know I'm just one person, but I do feel the weight of this commitment of wearing a visible sign that I am a part of the Muslim community.

I explain this to young women that, once you put on the scarf, your life does change. When people see you out in public, if you make a bad impression out there like you're rude to someone—well, the people who might see that misbehavior in public don't think: Oh, there's a rude woman. Because of the headscarf, they think: Oh, there's a rude Muslim!

This is a life-changing decision. It is a real responsibility to be a Muslim in America. I can't believe that it has been six years since the Hajj. A lot has happened over that time, but a lot is still the same. I still volunteer at school and in my community. I have taken a greater role in publicly representing the beauty of my faith—to correct the many common misconceptions about Islam.

My relationship with my Creator has grown stronger and has given me the inner peace I need to get through life. My headscarf is just another step in my spiritual journey.

CHAPTER 13

Teri Weingarden
Extending Our Hospitality

"Wait! Don't forget the bread! We want everyone to feel welcome!"

Teri Weingarden is a leader in her community, serving as treasurer for West Bloomfield Township, north of Detroit. She also is a professional communicator, a volunteer and an active member of Temple Shir Shalom. While she is passionate about her faith and Jewish traditions, she also learned at an early age from her family that extending hospitality to friends and neighbors is an essential part of her spiritual calling.

MY GREAT-GRANDPARENTS WERE immigrants and very religious. But once they had passed away my grandparents stopped keeping the Jewish dietary laws and approached Judaism in a more secular way. They celebrated all the major holidays to some extent. For example, they did not fast on Yom Kippur, but always enjoyed a break-the-fast dinner. They did not belong to a temple, but loved celebrating *simchas*, happy life cycle events such as bar mitzvahs and weddings. While they weren't religious they were still proud to be Jewish.

My grandpa grew up very poor. He was bright but did not excel in school since his family was too poor to purchase the textbooks. He would borrow books when he could, but was not able to reach his full potential in the classroom. Even at a young age, he had to work to help keep his household afloat. Through the years, he always did what he could to preserve the family. At one desperate point in the Great Depression, he told us, he was even driven to steal food for his family. As a young man, he would play pool for money. He was often struggling, but he was providing for his wife and three daughters.

I think the fact that he worked so hard for every dollar was a big part of why he so enjoyed sharing his money with his grandchildren. He would sometimes tell us, "When I get paid, you get paid," and give us a little money. He understood the struggle of poverty and did not want his grandchildren to experience poverty.

My grandpa was a voracious reader of books and newspapers and was current on every topic. He was a proud Democrat who believed in hard work and helping others. This was part of my grandfather's Jewish identity. He was the son of immigrants, working hard to provide for a better life in this country.

My grandma, one of three girls, grew up in a Jewish home. She was also a product of the Great Depression and would always have a plastic bag with her on walks for cans and bottles she found, to collect the deposit. She loved baking homemade apple pies so we would walk to the local grocery store, which was built on an old apple orchard. We would climb the tree outside the store for the best apples for our pie, never stepping inside the store.

I still remember watching my grandma set the table for Passover: the seder plate, wine glasses, salt water, a sweet chopped apple salad called *charoset*, celery, and a few baskets of matzah—the unleavened flatbread that the Bible instructs us to eat during Passover.

Then, at some point, my grandma would look over the table and say, "Wait! Don't forget the bread!" And by that, she meant regular bread, which wasn't supposed to be in our house at all during Passover. Grandma always explained this strange addition to our seder table this way: "We want everyone to feel welcome!" Yes, this was a Passover seder, and avoiding leavened bread was an essential part of the holiday, but my grandma wanted to ensure that our non-Jewish guests would feel warmly welcomed. She knew that for non-Jews, it wasn't a full meal without bread.

We would welcome family, friends and neighbors to our Passover table, some Jewish, some not, but all brought a hearty appetite. The room buzzed with multiple lively conversations all occurring simultaneously. We would always plan to do the entire service, but would end up doing just a small part, with everyone around the table taking a turn at reading. We would sing our favorite songs. Then we would eat until we were bursting.

When my grandparents could no longer host, my parents took over the family dinners. Our dinners always included Aunt Sue's family. Although Aunt Sue was not my biological aunt, she was both my parents' dearest friend. Aunt Sue had two sons, Eric and Jason, around the same age as my brother and I, and we were all friends from birth. Although devoted Catholics, they always participated enthusiastically in the seders because they enjoyed being a part of our traditions.

Every year we sang loudly, "Let My People Go," to commemorate the exodus from Egypt. So many deep memories were wrapped up in those dinners. Jewish families follow a Haggadah booklet during the seder and I can remember our family still having some of the tattered old Maxwell House Haggadahs, a nostalgic part of the holiday ever since the coffee company began publishing them as a promotion in the 1930s. Later, we included booklets made by my own children in their Jewish preschool class. Many of the songs and hand-drawn pictures were childish, but we just laughed and sang along. Aunt Sue and her boys sang loud and proud; celebrating each other's holidays was a part of our family connection.

In turn, we went to Aunt Sue's house for Christmas. We celebrated her family's holiday with a sparkling tree adorned with homemade ornaments, family heirlooms and beloved keepsakes. If I had questions about Christianity and the differences and similarities to Judaism, Aunt Sue was always willing to explain with a Bible in hand. She was a devote Catholic but respected our religious differences and truly believed we would all be together in the afterlife. Her explanations of Catholicism helped me understand the significance of her religion and reaffirmed my own faith.

Their Christmas tradition was to have a birthday cake for Jesus. When I was around 10 years old I mentioned this tradition to a friend at my Sunday Hebrew school. She was surprised that I would sing "Happy Birthday" to Jesus.

"After all, aren't you Jewish?" she asked.

That year at Christmas I was nervous on the car ride to Auntie Sue's house. I kept thinking about my friend's question. Could a Jewish girl sing a heartfelt round of "Happy Birthday" to Jesus? But as I looked around at the smiling faces of family and close friends, I realized this was the true meaning behind the holiday. Just as they attended our Passover seders, we could enjoy and celebrate their festivities. In my family, holidays were meant to be celebrations shared with close friends and family regardless of their religious background.

CHAPTER 14

The Rev. Amy Morgan
What We Did at Summer Camp

A sudden concern arose in me. Was I OK with this?

Navigating a new adult friendship is a challenge, but bigger surprises arise when friendships extend to our children. The Rev. Amy Morgan is a minister in the Presbyterian Church (USA). She is a graduate of Princeton Theological Seminary and New York University's Tisch School  of the Arts. In 2011, Amy co-authored the book, *The Girlfriends' Clergy Companion*. She is a past board member of WISDOM and is Yucatan Peninsula Mission board vice president. Amy and her husband, Jason, have a son, Dean.

FOR ME, SUMMERTIME means assembling a complicated puzzle of child care, camps, and activities for my son to cover the desert of boredom that stretches from mid-June to Labor Day. So I was thrilled when I got a call from my friend Serene one evening in July asking if my son, Dean, would like to come to her son's Bring a Friend to Camp Day. One more puzzle piece clicked into place! I couldn't say yes fast enough.

Dean was excited to see Ibrahim. They had become friends as Serene and I had: through our interfaith work with WISDOM. But we'd also arranged playdates when they were younger and attended a Tigers' game together, building friendships that deepened beyond any interfaith agenda.

But then Dean asked what sort of camp this was. Was it like his sleep-away camp, with outdoor activities and crafts and singing? Or more like our church's Vacation Bible School, with games and snacks and Bible stories? I thought about it. The camp was at Ibrahim's Montessori school, which happens to also be religiously affiliated with the Islamic faith. I told Dean that it was probably more like Vacation Bible School, but I wasn't sure if it would have a religious component or not.

As we dropped the boys off the next morning, Serene confided that Ibrahim was worried about Dean. He wondered if Dean would be all right with the Islamic studies portion of the day. Serene said, "I told him, 'Of course Dean will be fine. He's Amy's son!'"

I shared her confidence that Dean would have no problem, but a sudden concern arose in me. Was *I* okay with this? I hadn't given much thought to my son actually learning about Islam at camp. My concern was not about Dean losing his Christian faith or becoming confused or learning something contrary to our beliefs. I had learned enough about Islam from Serene and other wonderful Muslim friends that I knew Dean and I could have meaningful discussions about what he learned and draw connections to our faith that would help him grow. I had come to see Islam as a religion of peace and wisdom.

My concern was much more shallow. Was it crazy for a Christian pastor to send her son to an Islamic Montessori school?

What would people think? What did *I* think? When the invitation had been extended, I had just been eager to put together another piece of the summer puzzle picture. What this experience would mean on a larger scale hadn't even crossed my mind.

I finally reasoned that, since it was Bring a Friend to Camp Day, there were probably lots of other non-Muslim kids at the camp. Other parents had seen fit to send their children to camp that day. This wasn't anything momentous.

Later that afternoon, I picked Dean up from camp. The teacher who greeted me at the door gave Dean the highest compliment a Montessori teacher could give: "Your son is very creative." Dean was carrying a small, decorated cardboard box with tubes and pipe cleaners protruding from it.

"It's a zombie apocalypse-stopper," he explained.

Nothing out of the ordinary there, I thought as we got into the car.

I asked Dean about his day, and he told me, "It was fun." They played outside. He liked the lunch. Ibrahim had made a zombie apocalypse-stopper in "craft time," too.

"What about the Islamic studies?" I asked him. He told me they had a lesson, which he didn't remember much about (no different from Vacation Bible School). They prayed in Arabic, which he thought was interesting, but he didn't understand it. And then he and some of the other kids went out to the playground while the students from the school finished their lesson.

"So there were other kids there who aren't Muslim?" I asked.

"Oh no," Dean replied, "I was the only kid who wasn't Muslim."

Two possibilities occurred to me. Either no other non-Muslim parent in their right mind would send their child to an Islamic day camp, or none of the other students at this school chose to invite their non-Muslim friends to camp. I will never know which of those two possibilities represent the truth of the situation, but I suspect that the latter is the stronger candidate. And the more I thought about it, the more it sunk in just how momentous this day had been.

Interfaith relationships have been part of my son's upbringing since he was in pre-school. When he met Ibrahim, I was waiting with some trepidation for the inevitable question: "What's your mom wearing on her head?" But the question never came. Dean has accepted all my friends and acquaintances of other faiths at face value. They are Mommy's friends. They are good people. That's all he's ever needed to know.

I came to see this as a gift, but I had also taken it for granted. It wasn't until Dean told me that he was the only non-Muslim student at Bring a Friend to Camp Day that it hit me just how blessed I am, and he is, to have true friends of other faith traditions. Friends who would be brave enough to invite you to their camp for the day. Friends who I wouldn't think twice about trusting that this would be a good experience for my son.

I asked Dean what it was like being the only Christian, the only non-Muslim student at the camp. He said, "It was like normal."

May it always be so.

CHAPTER 15

Mona Farroukh
The Tiny Mighty

To live in the land of the free is one thing, but to actually live the life of the free is another.

Mona, Muslim from birth, found an all-too-common barrier preventing her from reaching out more widely in her community: an abusive spouse. Ending her marriage finally freed her to imagine how much larger her network of relationships could be. She now is a leader in her community, speaking about her experiences to help other women.

I LOVE THIS country. I can come and go as I please, laugh when I want, and do what I enjoy. But there was a day, even though I lived here in the United States, when embracing these freedoms was impossible. I am so glad that day is behind me.

I grew up knowing I wanted to make my mother proud. She raised my sister and me on her own—a single mother in Beirut, Lebanon, raising her daughters in the midst of a civil war. My heart ached to honor her, to justify the sacrifices she made for my sister and me. But not until I'd been married for 16 years did I realize that I would have to divorce my husband in order to live the life I envisioned for myself. Abuse is a widespread captor. For years, I endured because I thought it was best to keep the family together. Finally, however, I decided that keeping my family together was not protecting anyone, but instead was hurting us all.

Divorcing my husband was taboo in my Muslim community, as was speaking out about abuse. In ending my marriage, I also shed my *hijab*, a traditional head covering for many Muslim women. Removing that veil, a symbol which, to me, represented the voiceless and painful darkness in which I had lived for 16 years, was like lifting the curtain to my soul. The woman that had been locked inside for so long was finally set free.

My newfound freedom was not without conflict, though.

My mother taught me that people are good and are the same beneath their apparent differences. She taught me that I could accomplish anything, and she made my sister and me attend school, which was not required for girls in Lebanon. My mother also taught me that I am worthy—that my life has meaning. For a while, these beliefs lay dormant in my life. Finally, they could blossom and make me the woman I am today.

I returned to school, completing my bachelor's degree. This was wonderful. Many teachers inspired me, and one in particular helped me to see the world from new perspectives. I began to understand more about my role in the world.

After graduating with my bachelor's, I began working. My desire now is to help improve the health and well-being of the men, women and children of the Arab-American community. I strive to empower others, to plant in them the beliefs that my mother implanted in me. I am blessed to be able to do this work.

In 2007 I was awarded the Spirit Award by the Wayne County Prosecutor's Office. People in my community call me the "Tiny Mighty"—tiny, in that I stand less than five feet tall, and mighty, in that I am driven to give a voice to the voiceless. I have also been called "Phoenix," one who rose from the ashes with determination to live and to provide a decent life for her children. I've been called "The Lotus Flower," a symbol of rebirth. Such acknowledgement only encourages me to aim higher. I am now back in school, obtaining my master's and hoping to study for my Ph.D. My dream is to become an inspirational public speaker on empowering communities, especially for women.

To live in the land of the free is one thing, but to actually live the life of the free is another.

I no longer dream of honoring my mother. It now is a part of my everyday life—all I have to do is choose, each day, to make her proud.

Now, I know that can be done.

CHAPTER 16

Betty Sheehan
All the Same in Our Souls

My mother opened the door—and I will never forget her face! She looked stunned. Why wouldn't she talk to Favor? This was my best friend.

Betty Sheehan is a Catholic director of religious education. She also has worked with incarcerated teens. Her strong belief in justice and peace led her to become an active member in interfaith groups. She and her husband Bob have nine children and seven grandchildren.

"WE WANT YOU back! We want you back!" I heard my mother say.

I was 5 years old and unconscious from a fever so high my family thought I had died. With my sense of hearing taken over with my mother's cries, I had a vision. (I never told anyone in my family but my grandmother. Why? I don't know. You always share with your grandma.) But there in the grip of that fever I had a vision—of the Blessed Virgin Mother. There she was before me—her palms were open to me and I reached out to take her hands. But as I reached for her, she raised her palms.

"No," She said. "You can't come yet. It's too soon."

From that moment, I felt that vision was a call to me. Calling me to do God's work in whatever way I can. In my Catholic faith I'm known as one who is kind of different. Maybe it's because I felt I was called. Maybe it's because of the way I approach life. Maybe it's because I never had to overcome accepting people of other races or cultures. We are all the same within our souls. I've never felt any other way.

I am the director of the religious education program at my church, and it is my belief that religious education works when the students feel positive reinforcement through praise and acknowledgment—and there are parents, guardians or grandparents who set a primary example for their children by their own faith actions. We have volunteers who willingly give of their time to share in the ministry of "echoing the Word of God." There's not an age of a child I do not love!

Because these children are our progeny, I realize that passing on religious traditions takes the whole community. It is my prayer that when setting up programs, I never forget the importance of inclusion, because we are all the same within our souls and justice and peace will only occur if it begins with us.

I've gone to two Sister Circles and what amazed me both times was how all of us came together—we had Hindu women, Muslim, Bahá'í, a Roman Catholic like me, a Jewish woman. The topic of one evening was anger. I sat back and listened to all the conversations, and I'm telling you, everything they said was common to us all. We all have hurts; we all have angers. We're all seeking love and forgiveness, and the way we choose to seek love and forgiveness—the way we express it—is what makes us different. But if you sit back and listen, we're all saying the same things. The Abrahamic story is for everyone. I realized there is no difference in faith; our souls all have the same struggles. At least, that's how I've always approached life.

Nothing I do is on my own; I don't feel I am an entity unto myself. Each day I pray, "God, let me do Your work this day." When I speak to teens and children, I pray, "God, let my words be Your words. Let Your words work through me." I work with teens who have attempted suicide. I think the no. 1 cause for these attempts is that these children believe that no one is there for them. Someone who knows they are special. If they can just believe there is one God, Allah, the Most High, they won't give up.

Same with the elderly. I think a lot of times the elderly are simply misdiagnosed. What is diagnosed as depression is the feeling that they are no longer valued. They are lost—a forgotten generation. We don't realize the beauty and history that they can share. That's why I invite my grandmothers to come in and help in ways they feel comfortable (reading, listening to prayers, baking). That's why I bring my teens in to help the younger classes. Every person has value. Every person has something to give.

So here's what I do with my Confirmation students. I pair them up with an elderly person in the parish, someone 70 or 80 years old. They do not meet at first, but are simply given each other's names and are told to pray for each other. Come Thanksgiving, I have the teens make a meal for their prayer friend. That's when they meet for the first time. And when they are confirmed, their senior buddy packs them a lunch and writes them a letter.

Like I said, every person on this Earth has value. Every person has something to give.

When my husband's work transferred us to Mexico, the generosity I witnessed stayed with me long after we moved to Detroit. In Mexico, people were poor as heck but they opened their homes to us. They shared what they had. It was culture shock for my kids, let me tell you. My 6-year-old couldn't understand it. Seeing 4-year-olds begging was shocking! One day, my daughter saw a barefoot child and tried to take off her own shoes to give them to the child. I think those years in Mexico are the reason all four of my children are very much givers. You can't come back from there and say, "I have nothing," when we are so blessed. I have lights in my home I can turn on. I know my house will be warm in the winter. I have clean water to drink.

I think that you are somewhere for a reason, a reason why things happen.

I have been out to the New Mexico desert and have visited the tribe called the "Corn Huskers," and to Canada to visit the Chippewas. What may appear as different is truly the same. The Native American tribe danced with corn—dressed only in corn husks–and passed out loaves of cornbread. Yet, what was so apparent was the common thread of "sharing and breaking bread among others."

The Eucharistic bread, in my Catholic faith, is considered the source and summit of coming to the table. The Canadian tribe celebrated with the "Prayer to the Four Winds," a prayer which gives thanks, adoration and praise to the Creator for the circle of life and its blessings. It, too, parallels the Catholic faith's acknowledgment of God's grace through the Sacraments, which celebrates the life given to us by God.

Ceremonies may certainly differ, but if we are going to come together in this world, we have to have acceptance before understanding. If we can't open our doors in our personal communities to people who are different because of their color or creed, how can we expect nations to do so?

Here's a story about opening doors. It happened to me in first grade:

My best friend's name was Favor. I told my mother all about her, how we ate lunch together every day, and—could I please bring her home with me? What I didn't tell her, because I hadn't realized it, was that Favor was black.

The day came, and Favor and I walked home from school. My mother opened the door—and I will never forget her face! She looked stunned. Why wouldn't she talk to Favor? This was my best friend.

We played the whole afternoon, and after she left, my mother said, "You can't bring her back anymore. If she comes again, people will talk." I knew right away there was something wrong with that.

Only years later did I learn, from my aunt, that four African-American girls had once jumped my mother on a bus and tried to rob her. That's when I realized she had been afraid for me all those years ago. My mother was a warm and giving person, always reaching out to people. Her reaction to Favor was so out of character. All I knew that afternoon was she didn't like my friend.

You have to be open with children. If my mother had been open with me, she might have been able to see Favor as I did: she was my friend. I would have had the opportunity to talk about it, and talking at least opens the door to conversation. But to be open, you first must recognize your fears and then ask yourself if your fears are justified or are only misconceptions. Maybe my mother would have understood what life has taught me—we are all the same in our souls.

Chapter 17

Padma Kuppa
Sharing Religious Ideals, American Ideals

When we are at our best as people, we are able to see our communities and our world as a loving family.

Padma is a community activist on behalf of diversity and education, especially in the areas of faith and culture. She was born in 1965 in India, moved to the United States as a child and grew up in a home where education was highly valued. As an adult, she has worked as  an information-technology consultant and also actively supports the Hindu temple in Troy, a city north of Detroit, in Michigan. After a lifetime as a proud American herself, Padma was surprised by one of her first public encounters with American neighbors of other faiths.

ONE OF MY favorite Bible verses is from 1 Corinthians: "Faith, hope and love abide, these three; and the greatest of these is love." This is a lot like passages in Hindu scriptures, including these words from the Maha Upanishad: "The whole world is a family." There also is a prayer of peace in the Rig Veda that reads, in English: "May all be happy. May all be healthy. May all be prosperous. Let no one suffer."

I'm a mom in a "typical" American family—like millions of other families in our country. We share common hopes for a happy, healthy life. My husband is an automotive engineer. My kids play baseball and soccer. My daughter has been a Girl Scout; my son has been a Cub Scout.

I try to serve my community as well as my own house of worship. A number of years ago, I agreed to serve on Troy's Ethnic Issues Advisory Board, a group of 10 people appointed by the City Council. That's one of the reasons I got involved in the National Day of Prayer.

When I first heard about Troy's annual public gathering for the annual National Day of Prayer event in 2004, I didn't know much about its history, but the idea of joining in prayer once a year sounded great to me. I didn't want to serve as the Hindu representative. I just hoped that the organizers would call the Hindu temple and invite someone who could represent our faith among all the other faiths that would be represented on the steps of City Hall that day. If they needed help finding someone, I was happy to ask around. I know quite a few people in the Hindu community.

But, as it turned out, no one called our temple. I was told that all the details for the Troy event in 2004 were already planned. I began to realize that there was no place in the Troy schedule for a Hindu to pray: we were being denied the right to participate in a program of prayer right there, on the steps of our own City Hall.

I sent an email to the City Council, expressing my concern about this. As a result, the mayor called me and said, "Padma, you can come and, during my opening remarks, you can say a Hindu prayer."

She was very welcoming to me that day, and said to the crowd of about 100 men, women and children: "Now, someone from our Ethnic Issues Advisory Board will say a few words."

From my place—standing beside side of the mayor—I slowly stepped over to the microphone. I was anxious to be addressing a crowd and, as I began to pray, I was so focused on the prayer itself that I wasn't focusing too much on the faces of the people standing in front of me. I simply used the four-line peace prayer from the Rig Veda. I recited it in Sanskrit and then in English. I didn't invoke any name. I didn't say, "Let's pray in the name of X, Y or Z." I just used the four simple lines of a prayer that people everywhere should be able to share.

But, as I stepped back, I could sense that most of the people didn't really want me there. I recall a Bahá'í friend trying to reassure me with supportive words, but it became clear that this crowd didn't like my being there. I didn't leave after my prayer was finished. I participated in the whole program, which took about an hour. When the group prayed the Lord's Prayer, I prayed along.

As I talked with a few people afterward, I began to realize that this crowd was made up mainly of conservative Christians. Some of the children who attended the event were home-schooled. People were passing out literature from evangelical groups.

Finally, I thought: Boy, I shouldn't have come here today. I felt out of place and alone. I didn't realize that such opposition existed in my own community to people of other faiths.

I'm not naïve. I've always known that Michigan isn't as inclusive a place as my native New York. I still remember walking up to a counter at a place of business in Troy when a blonde, Caucasian woman walked up shortly after I got there. The person behind the counter turned to this woman and, without even acknowledging me, began to take care of her business first. Another time, my daughter wasn't invited to the birthday party of a good friend from school because this friend had chosen a Vacation Bible School theme for her party. My daughter was hurt that her friends had excluded her.

But it wasn't until 2005 that I realized how much some people in my own community hate the idea of allowing people of other faiths to take part in public events. I support our American ideals of freedom of speech and freedom of religion. We don't have to allow everyone into our houses of worship. We're free to express ourselves and our different faiths. But when someone plans to use a public place like the steps of City Hall for an official event that claims to represent our government and our whole community—that's different.

At first—in the months before that 2005 National Day of Prayer—I tried to get involved in the planning process for the event. Then, in March of that year, one City Council meeting got very ugly when the issue of diversity at these events was raised. As often happens with this kind of heated political issue, some activists from outside of our city had been brought in to try to argue the case for keeping a limitation on the National Day of Prayer.

I will never forget the experience of a man from an outside legal-advocacy center standing up and yelling at me—right there in my own hometown. He made me feel so little! He spoke to me as if to say: Why can't we crush you, this little bug, under our feet? I was stunned. I thought: If God created all of us, how can someone ever treat another human like that in God's name? You don't have to accept my beliefs. I don't have to accept your beliefs. But why can't we add our good wishes together, if we're going to share our prayers for the whole city? How could this man get so angry that he would treat me so hatefully? America has many faiths and also people of no faith, as well. All of us should feel welcome where we live.

In Troy, I hit a brick wall with this National Day of Prayer organization. At first, I didn't realize how closely its history is associated with conservative Christian political movements. At one point in 2005, I went online and got involved in an Internet chat with James Towey, the head of the office of faith-based initiatives for President George Bush. I asked Mr. Towey how President Bush observes the National Day of Prayer, and he said, "Oh, the President does it in a very diverse way!" And he pointed me to this document I could print out that showed how the White House includes many faiths in its observance. I thought that the document was the proof we needed to open things up in Troy. Everyone thought of President Bush as a conservative Christian, but he was inclusive in his expression of the National Day of Prayer.

Of course, nothing happened initially, in 2005. A long and complicated series of events unfolded that spring and, as a direct result, I became very active in helping to form a new organization, which is called the Troy Interfaith Group. That first spring, the Troy Interfaith Group had a diverse service that drew 250 people, including the city's mayor. She was threatened with a recall for supporting us, but that effort failed.

Since 2005, our group has grown and we have supported many programs that have inspired other people across the United States. In 2007, for example, our group was lifted up as an example by Harvard's Pluralism Project.

This whole journey started, for me, with my surprise in discovering that some of my neighbors did not want me to pray with them on the steps of our City Hall in the name of our City of Troy.

That's simply not the American ideal. When we are at our best as people, we are able to see our communities and our world as a loving family. I grew up celebrating holidays with friends of various faith traditions. When I was heading to college, my father gave me three books: the Bible, the Baghavad Gita and the complete works of William Shakespeare. He told me: "The world's great truths are in these three books."

I do believe there are certain truths all people can share—and one of them is that no one should make anyone else feel like "the other" in his or her own hometown. As a mom, I certainly don't want my children growing up feeling that way.

I realize that India isn't perfect in dealing with diversity. In India, people often are torn apart by socio-economic and religious stratification. America isn't perfect, either, but the United States is supposed to be a place in the world where everyone can be accepted for who he or she is.

I'd be disappointed with myself if I *didn't* try to defend that American ideal. And although I may sound like a red-white-and-blue flag waver, I don't think that's such a bad thing if it helps us to remember who we're supposed to be in the world.

Part IV

Spiritual Transitions

Today, 4 out of 10 Americans are practicing a faith different than the one in which they were raised, according to Pew Research. Such spiritual transitions are not easy! If we make a personal pilgrimage from one faith to another, what will our friends think?

CHAPTER 18

Noelle Sutherland
New Friends and Old Friends

*I'm human. I get afraid. I don't want
to ruin things with friends.*

Noelle grew up in a household
with little interest in religion,
but she became curious as a
teenager and sampled a wide
range of religious experiences.
When she got married in 2002
and started her own family, she
and her husband decided to
make religious practice a central part of their home. They joined
a little-known religious group within Buddhism. What happens
when, as an adult, you become a part of a small religious group?
What happens with old friends when your life changes and you
meet new friends?

I HAVE SOME friends who have been extremely accepting about our religion. They've seen how much it has changed my life in positive ways. They've asked questions about it, and I'm happy to answer their questions. But mostly these are friends I've met more recently—friends who haven't known me for years. There are old friends who I still haven't told that I'm now Buddhist.

My husband and I follow Nichiren Daishonin Buddhism, and most of the followers worldwide are Japanese. I'm not. I'm Caucasian. I grew up in the Midwest. My family has lived in Michigan forever. So, this is quite different for people who knew me years ago while I was growing up.I have a master's degree and I'm a middle-school teacher of science and social studies. I hadn't really found a religion for myself, but my husband and I—as we met and eventually got married—discovered that we both had this strong connection with Buddhism and the various philosophies and practices within Buddhism. We had both been reading about it, we discovered! My husband had a whole collection of books about Buddhism. While I hadn't had any religious upbringing, he came from a family that was very strongly Roman Catholic. So, this was new and quite different for both of us—but we both felt this very strong connection to Buddhism.

We had not really acted on that, but when we were married I got pregnant right away. We both realized: We've got a family coming—we should go ahead and find someplace to attend. We began trying different churches, and one day we met some people who were practicing Nichiren Buddhism. Very quickly we found that—my gosh—everything about their practice was exactly what we were looking for.

We became Nichiren Buddhist about six years ago. Nichiren Daishonin was a Japanese monk born in Japan in 1222. Basically, we follow the *Lotus Sutra*, writings of Nichiren Diashonin, and chant *Nam-myoho-renge-kyo* daily. Buddhism is a mainstream religion, and Nichiren Buddhism is growing in size, but there aren't a lot of people who practice this in Michigan.

We practice in our homes, where we also hold meetings. We also attend monthly meetings at a community center. We have potlucks. You might think that my son, growing up in the suburbs, would be getting a steady diet of pizza and hamburgers. But, because most of the people in Nichiren Buddhism are from Asia, my son is growing up eating curry and sushi regularly.

This choice we've made has been absolutely wonderful for my husband and our family, but it has been a struggle for me in other ways. We live in a mostly Christian society in this country, and I guess a lot of people don't realize how important the Asian influence has become. Millions of Americans are practicing yoga, and Asian religious traditions are a growing part of this country's culture—but some people are not very accepting of our choice.

I've had people look at me and say: "You're an American Caucasian woman—so how can you be a Buddhist?"

Even though we've spent years with our religious practice, I still haven't worked out how to relate to all of my old friends. There are still some who knew me years ago who I haven't talked with about this. I'm not sure of what their reactions would be.

This has been a very good choice for us. People who know me can see that I've got a lot more optimism about life now, but there is a fear in some friendships. I'm human. I get afraid. I don't want to ruin things with friends. I do wonder: Will I be judged by a different standard if this person knows my religious experiences are not the same as most people?

It's a lot easier for me to form new friendships. When I make new friends, things aren't so difficult. I just describe who I am. This is all just a part of my life. New friends get to know the person I am today. Buddhism is a large part of my life, and I don't find that I need to explain myself, only explain what they might not know about my religion.

What I fear is that someone I knew in the past won't respect the importance of my choices. I don't want to hear them saying, "Oh, this is just a phase you're going through." And, I don't want to hear them say, "Oh, it's just a bandwagon she's jumping on."

In some ways, I wish I had been born into Buddhism. There's a phrase, "fortune babies"—for people who were born and grew up in the religion. When you're born into it, you've got all the confidence and all the knowledge of your tradition from so many years of living within it.

But there are a lot of Americans like me, who look around for the religion that's right for them—and who do make changes. Millions of Americans are making new religious choices. I hope that more people will become accepting of these choices.

I know it's possible. At a wedding, I found myself sitting at a table with a girlfriend from college. She's a Christian but she is very open to new ideas. We got to talking about what we believe. I told her about my practice—and she was interested in my story. We had a good and very lengthy discussion. She made me feel confident in the way she responded. It was a wonderful experience.

I wish people would stay open-minded, like this friend I met again at the wedding. The key is acceptance. I don't like the word "tolerate." As a teacher, I can "tolerate" kids at school, but that's not enough for strong relationships between friends. We need more than that in our relationships. Acceptance truly helps to make our lives better.

CHAPTER 19

Victoria Freile
A New Faith in a Traditional Family

Would I cause them even greater suffering with my own announcement?

Victoria Freile was born in Ecuador to a Catholic family. She was 31 when she became a Baháʼí and moved to Dar es Salaam, Tanzania. After two years, she moved to Michigan where she currently resides with her family. She has three daughters and currently works as a Parent Resource Assistant for families in the Waterford School District in which English is their second language.

THE LAND OF my birth is predominantly Catholic, and I grew up in a home with parents who taught my siblings and me their faith from as long as I can remember. We went to Catholic schools and attended Mass every Sunday. Everyone I knew was Catholic.

My spiritual journey was influenced by a dream that eventually led me toward the Bahá'í faith—a dream so vivid that I remember it to this day. At the time, I was 19 and a student of architecture at the Catholic University of Santiago de Guayaquil. There were many components to my dream. In essence, I was seeing and hearing special celestial events in which people from many different ethnic and religious backgrounds were walking together. They were saying that their prophet had returned.

I could not keep this dream to myself. My best friend was Pablo, a fellow architecture student and also a very devoted Catholic. I told him about my dream. For a while, the dream receded into the back of my mind. But my relationship with Pablo deepened and eventually we married. We had two little girls. Years passed.

While the girls were still quite young and we were visiting my sister Cecilia, I wound up talking with my brother-in-law Marcelo who was a Bahá'í. During that visit and those conversations, I realized that my dream was connected with the universal principles and prophecies of the Bahá'í faith—especially that Baha'u'llah represents the return of the prophets foretold in other world religions.

My parents began to worry when several of us in the family moved toward the Bahá'í faith. In 1992, Pablo decided to become a Bahá'í. This shocked my parents who knew Pablo as a strong Catholic. Three months later, my sister Cecilia also decided to become a Bahá'í, causing more unease in the family—one of their daughters was moving away from the family's traditional faith. Next, my sister Diana started dating a Bahá'í friend.

My parents were really concerned and wondered if they had done something wrong in our upbringing. Their anxiety over these changes made me hesitant to publicly declare that, in my heart, I was a Bahá'í, too. I was torn, thinking about my relationship with my parents. Would I cause them even greater suffering with my own announcement?

Almost three years passed from the time Pablo declared his new faith. My daughters, Diana and Andrea, loved the Bahá'í faith by the time they were 8 and 7. On a Sunday in October 1995, I decided to officially declare as a Bahá'í. At that point, my parents already had a strong suspicion that I was following this spiritual path.

I expected a response. I knew my parents were sensitive about this subject. But, my mother never said anything about it.

The real test for me came during my 10th wedding anniversary in March 1996, when Pablo and I decided to renew our vows by having a Bahá'í wedding ceremony. I came back to my parents and asked them to give me their blessing again.

To my surprise, they were very open and supportive. I knew it wasn't easy for my mother, but nevertheless she accepted my decision and helped me get ready for the ceremony and shared my joy and spiritual celebration.

In June 1996 we moved to Tanzania, Africa, for a job opportunity. After two years, we moved to Michigan and have lived here since. Throughout the years my mother and I have visited each other and have had the opportunity to share wonderful times together. On occasion, she has lived with us for an extended period such as the months after I gave birth to my youngest daughter, Jessica, in November 2000.

Whenever we have the chance to spend time together, wonderful things have happened. For example, as a family we have continued to pray together before going to bed. This is a tradition we have had from the time I was a kid. My mother was open to sharing Catholic prayers with us as well as reciting Bahá'í prayers.

On Sundays I would accompany her to church and in many instances when we had Bahá'í gatherings in our house she not only participated but welcomed my Bahá'í friends and made them feel at home. I love my parents. My relationship with my mother throughout the years has become stronger because there is respect and acceptance. I know it is difficult for a Catholic believer to see someone leave that faith—especially if that person is a son or daughter.

What I have learned through these experiences is that my mother was able to recognize the harmony that characterizes my marriage and our family—and she knows that believing in God goes beyond any religious boundaries and is more about actions than words.

When I go back in time and think about what concerned me the most about becoming a Bahá'í, it was a fear of my parents' reaction. I was especially concerned about how my decision would affect my relationship with my mother. Now, in retrospect, I realize my fears were unfounded. My mother's unconditional love was strong enough that our family remains united even through this spiritual transition.

CHAPTER 20

Karla Joy Huber
Creating a New Definition of Blended Family

It is no coincidence that both the Bahá'í faith and SGI Nichiren Buddhism share a common motto: "Unity in diversity."

In the previous chapter, Victoria Freile tells the story of stresses within her family as she and her husband moved toward the Bahá'í faith. Millions of Americans move through religious conversions from one faith to another and, in this story, Karla Huber tells about concerns as she moved away from the Bahá'í faith. Karla is a writer, tutor and artist who specializes in writing about interfaith relations and holistic health. She is a practicing Nichiren Buddhist who shares her Buddhist and interfaith insights about "thinking spiritually and culturally outside the box" at www.karlahuberblog.blogspot.com.

BEFORE I WAS a Buddhist, I was a Bahá'í for 12 years. During that time, I blended pieces from various religions to come up with a very customized—and rather isolated—personal spirituality. I didn't have a good system for dealing with life-changing challenges, such as the death of someone close to me. I reached a spiritual impasse shortly after my beloved Granddaddy Huber died, and spent the next month in a fog, not really sure what I wanted to do spiritually from that point.

Around that time, my friend Tony introduced me to Nichiren Buddhism, and soon after that I started studying with him and attending SGI Buddhist meetings. It didn't take me long to realize I had finally found the spiritual path with the practical dimension I needed to help me use my faith to truly change my whole life. One of the most significant things it's changed for me is how I relate with the people who are most important to me.

After I became Buddhist, I was apprehensive of how my Bahá'í friends would respond. Since I knew several of them read my online blog, I decided that was a good way to let everyone know. I wrote my "Buddhist coming-out" post in mid-2015 shortly before receiving the Gohonzon (the rite of passage for becoming Nichiren Buddhist), and linked it on my Facebook page to assure people would see it. Some Bahá'í friends read it and commented positively.

Great! I thought, *Mission accomplished.*

Then, a few months later, one of them told me he'd mentioned my becoming a Buddhist to a mutual friend, another Bahá'í— and she was surprised. Subsequent conversations with other Bahá'ís revealed that most of them, in fact, still did not know about my spiritual transition. The SGI Buddhist emblem on a necklace I wear even resembles the stylized Bahá'í star symbol from a distance, so even that didn't cue people that something was different.

I thought: *This means I'll have to have the potentially awkward conversations after all.*

Two of the people whose responses mattered the most to me were John and Christa. I became close with them in 2010 when they began hosting community socials at their home, which were open to anyone. As a host and friend, John had a knack for making everyone feel personally appreciated—like a parent welcoming his grown children home. I also had a few wonderful one-on-one conversations with Christa, in which she shared insights about relationships and about health and wellness that really had a profound effect on the way I approached some changes I needed to make in my life.

I wouldn't let anyone's opinion influence my decision about being Buddhist, but I told my best friend, Dan, that because John and Christa were like honorary parents to me, their opinions mattered very much. When Dan and I were on our way to have lunch with them in August 2015, I told him, "I feel like I'm coming out to my parents."

During lunch, I told them. They both looked mildly surprised for a moment, then their demeanor seemed like they simply updated their mental records of what they knew about me. John talked a bit about his understanding of Buddhism—then our conversation moved to other topics.

Flashing forward a few months, January 24, 2016 was the second-to-last time I saw John. He was in the hospital, getting stabilized enough to go home for his last days after a two-year battle with cancer. When John saw Dan and me enter his hospital room, he perked up and greeted us cheerfully.

John beckoned me close and said, "I have a question for you. Which one is yours: 'Nam-Myoho-Renge-Kyo,' or … " and he tried to name another Buddhist chant. I told him it was the first one, and he seemed pleased that he got it right.

I was deeply moved that at some point in the past few months of concluding his life, John had taken the time to find something central to Nichiren Buddhism to say to me. His welcoming question felt like the blessings adult offspring seek from their parents after making a life decision that is contrary to the family heritage.

A few weeks later, John's family asked me to read something Buddhist during the interfaith devotional-readings segment of his funeral. This was another demonstration of his family's acceptance of me that I will always cherish in my heart.

About a month after John's death, I was out with Dan and our friend Joe when they invited me to join them for dinner at the home of Jim and Louise, whose family is closely related to John's and Christa's by marriage. I was thrilled when Jim and Louise welcomed me as they always had, and I felt no shift in their demeanor toward me when the subject came up that I had become Buddhist since they last saw me. Their warm welcome and hospitality told me that they still saw me as the Karla they had always known, still an honorary member of their family.

Two other family friends in attendance were curious to hear about what brought me to Nichiren Buddhism, and we had a great dialogue about it. While some of what I said didn't accord with Bahá'í belief, at no point did I get the impression that I was alienating them with what I was saying. Interfaith relations have always been very important to Bahá'ís. Even the scriptural writings of the Bahá'í faith encourage such alliances for the sake of unity and harmony of the human race. *Soka Gakkai* Nichiren Buddhism also places great emphasis on interreligious dialogue, for the same reasons. Thus, I felt that the only thing that really changed in my relationship with my Bahá'í friends was simply that I had gone from being a fellow-Bahá'í to what Bahá'ís call a "friend of the faith." We now bond through the interfaith emphasis of our faiths rather than through our shared religious faith.

I've heard comments from a lot of people who move from one religion to another that indicate they have resentment toward their previous community or the whole religion. One common reason for this is the way they're treated in response to expressing views contrary to their earlier community. I felt that coming out to my Bahá'í friends would be a friendship test. Through the responses I've gotten, I realized how many unconditional friends I have.

In April 2017, Blair, whom I've known for 15 years, told me she'd just recently heard that I had become Buddhist. "I wasn't at all surprised!" she said. She told me she could always tell that I struggled on the Bahá'í path, and that when she heard I became Buddhist, she was happy for me. She looked me deep in the eyes and said she could see it was a good fit for me, and that I looked happy and radiant. I got a really warm feeling then, and I realized that when Blair looks me in the eyes, she's looking into my soul, in a way that tells me she really understands something very important about how I'm spiritually wired.

Somewhere in his religious studies, John said he'd found a reference to creating a "meta-community." By that phrase, he was describing a community that does not require common belief—or even any belief. I told him during our conversation in January 2016, "You made us all a family."

"That was my intent," he had replied.

My continued friendships within the Bahá'í community have taught me the importance of honoring my ties with all the people who have welcomed me into their hearts and homes, regardless of any religious differences, and of continuing to learn from their religions as well as from my own. I am glad that my karma has connected me with people who are such great examples of genuine friendship, and who are secure enough in their own beliefs that they do not feel threatened or alienated by the idea of someone leaving their ranks for another spiritual path.

It is no coincidence that both the Bahá'í faith and SGI Nichiren Buddhism share a common motto: "Unity in diversity."

CHAPTER 21

Delores Lyons
Marinated, Battered and Deep-Fried in Religion

I truly loved the sounds, energy and traditions of the black church.

Americans who leave Christianity for Eastern religions prompt concerns from friends and family—and that's especially true in black Protestant communities, according to Pew Research. The good news is that a friendly acceptance of Eastern faiths, including Buddhism, is growing nationwide. A 2017 Pew study found that 60 percent of all Americans now "feel warmly toward" Buddhists—a significant improvement in recent years. As a social worker, Delores Lyons has experienced that transition toward acceptance over many years. She has dedicated her life to helping people, often in cross-cultural settings. So, she was well aware of the challenges she would face as she made her own spiritual transition.

I OFTEN TELL people: I was marinated, battered and deep-fried in religion. That's because I grew up in a fundamental Christian home within the black Baptist tradition. Religion was my life. If my family wasn't in church or involved in a religious activity at home, Christian radio filled the gap. The radio played around the clock. I would go to sleep every night and awaken each morning to something religious.

One tradition in our home was "family devotion." Just before bedtime my mother, brother and I would gather around the old upright piano that was badly in need of tuning. Mother would begin playing and singing any one of her favorite hymns in a voice that was also badly in need of tuning. My older brother Hugh did not take kindly to my snickering at Mother's singing. If I showed any sign of amusement, he would sneak me the "evil eye" then join in with Mother, helping her to keep in tune. My part was to read Scripture. Mother would give a mini-sermon of sorts on handling life's challenges the Christian way. Hugh would pray, then we'd close out with another one of Mother's favorite hymns.

I loved our Christian way of life; and I truly loved the sounds, energy, and traditions of the black church. The interesting thing though, was that even though we were staunch Baptists, my mother was quite open to other religions. All anyone had to do is profess their belief in God, and Mother had no qualms sending me off with them to worship. Consequently, I found myself in mosques, synagogues, and churches with teachings drastically different from my own. We also held regular Bible studies at home with Jehovah's Witnesses, Mormons, and Seventh-day Adventists.

I believed that my Christian teachings provided everything I needed to navigate whatever problems the world dished out. College exposed me to activities and behaviors I had never encountered before—like wild parties, drugs, and alcohol. Fortunately, adherence to my faith helped me avoid those pitfalls. Nonetheless, I was not prepared for the challenges of becoming a single mom living far away from home, trying to navigate a high-profile career with no support system. The "Jesus will fix it for you" model did not seem to work when it came to the "isms" and "ists" of society. I eventually succumbed to the drop-kicks of life and fell into a state of depression. I sensed that there had to be more to understand and I started asking deeper questions. The spiritual answers that resonated came from outside the boundaries of my religion.

My gateway into Buddhism was through Metaphysics and New Thought teachings. I particularly loved the emphasis on what they called "practicing the silence"—a big difference from what I was used to in my Baptist church. At Detroit Unity Temple, I took part in some awesome guided meditations. One day, rather than a guided meditation, we were invited to keep focus on our breath—to concentrate on our breathing in, then our breathing out. That's all we did in complete silence for what may have been 10 or 15 minutes. All I know is I did not want that meditation to end.

That night I had a dream; I dreamt Jesus had introduced me to his best friend: Buddha. When I awoke, I felt that dream was telling me to go to a Buddhist temple—and I did. That was 23 years ago and I have been Buddhist ever since.

Reactions from Christians to my being Buddhist have varied over the years, particularly from those in the black church. Most of my friends accept my choice, but insist that they will *never* visit a temple. This is largely because of their impressions of what Buddhism represents and what Buddhists do. For example, because there are usually statues in Buddhist temples, many assume that Buddhists worship these statues.

One day, I got into a philosophical discussion with one of my closest friends that led to a vigorous dialogue about religion. My friend surprised me when he said he would come to the temple—although he said he was coming because it was his duty as a Christian to proselytize for his faith. I was anxious, of course, but I also was excited about his impending visit.

The Sunday arrived for his visit and we met at the temple. He was extremely nervous but I honored him for taking a major step in being willing to experience something different. We went through all the rituals of the service: the prostrations, the sitting, chanting, and finally a dharma talk given by the teacher. Afterwards we were served tea and treats. That was the time for questions and answers. I braced myself for the possibility of what my friend would say.

Instead, he listened intently to what everyone else was saying. As we left the temple, he made his bows to everyone—even gave and received a few hugs. Still appearing a bit stunned he said, "Everyone was so nice."

Weeks later, he told me he enjoyed the beautiful chants and meditation. He now lives on the West Coast and says Buddhist meditation is very much a part of his Christian life.

Part V

Not Enemies
After All

War seems to be a constant in our world. International observers report that more than 60 lethal conflicts continue to claim lives worldwide. Despite these horrors—friendships continue to blossom.

CHAPTER 22

Motoko F. Huthwaite
Views From the Enemy Camps

When the sirens went off again, we all went and sat in the air raid shelter expecting to die there. There was no stopping the atomic bombs if they hit.

In this section of the book, women are telling stories about mistaken impressions of people—fearing that someone might be an enemy. Motoko's story turns the perspective 180 degrees. While still a girl, she experienced the suspicion and enmity of two nations. Born  in Boston in 1927, Motoko's lifelong pursuit of education eventually led, in the 1970s, to a doctorate and professional expertise in children's literature. She remains deeply concerned about the quality of life for children and families around the world. She is a vigorous activist on behalf of ending nuclear weapons, promoting world peace and improving interfaith relations through her own lay leadership in the Presbyterian Church (USA).

I LIVED IN America when Pearl Harbor was attacked. So, in December 1941, I was perceived as the enemy in my hometown of Cambridge, Massachusetts.

I lived in Japan when the atomic bomb was dropped on Hiroshima—so, then, I was perceived as the enemy in my family's homeland, where my clothing, my language and even my particular style of wire-rimmed glasses made me stand out as the enemy—this time as one of the Americans who was dropping bombs.

I was an enemy in both of my countries.

When the war started in 1941, I was 14 years old and in the ninth grade. My father was an orthodontist who taught at Harvard. He had been living in the United States since the 1920s, but the Oriental Exclusion Act of 1924 prevented him from becoming an American citizen. I was born in the U.S. and so was my brother, who was in fourth grade, so we were both dual citizens of Japan and the U.S.

When news of the attack on Pearl Harbor came, only my brother and I were at home. We heard it first from a Japanese Harvard student who called the house. He asked for my parents. I told him they weren't home. Then, he said, "Japan and America are at war!"

I had no idea what to do. I called for my brother to come inside. We sat there, inside the house, until my parents came home.

When I told my parents the news, I remember them turning absolutely white. They were aghast. We turned on the radio and we were glued to the announcer's voice saying, over and over again, that Pearl Harbor had been attacked.

The big question in our household was: Do we go to school the next day?

My brother and I attended a small private school called Buckingham—and we did return to classes the next day. That school had an excellent program and I remember the principal said to the whole student body at an assembly: "There will be no war within the walls of this school."

My brother and I were the only Japanese children in the school. So everyone was looking at us.

The principal also talked individually to children who were our friends, and they understood that they needed to protect us. My best friends would sit in a circle around me. And my brother was surrounded by his friends at recess. One of his friends told other boys, quite loudly: "You touch him and I'll knock yer block off!"

But school wasn't the only place we had to go outside our home. Each week, I had to take a bus across the Charles River into Boston to my piano lesson. The first time I had to do that I sat there, so frightened, in my seat on the bus: If they realize that I am Japanese, what will they do to me? I wondered. And I worked out a plan in my head: If someone confronts me, I'll tell them I'm Chinese. They won't know the difference. But, there was no problem on the bus.

My parents faced far worse problems. One day, the police accosted my mother, claiming she was taking a photograph of a bridge; they had mistaken her rectangular-shaped purse for a camera. Then, my parents came home another day with funny stains on their fingers because they had been fingerprinted. The Japanese students at Harvard were in trouble. Some of my father's patients cancelled.

We got a telegram from the U.S. government that said: If you desire repatriation to Japan, report to Ellis Island at such-and-such a date. My parents carefully considered this, and they decided we were no longer welcome in the U.S. My father decided that he would stay and continue his dental practice and keep our apartment, but that my mother, my brother and I would go to Japan.

Do you know who stepped forward to help us at this very difficult time? Quakers. We were Buddhist and Shinto, like most Japanese families, and so I was absolutely bewildered to meet these people who called themselves Quakers. When other people were trying to kick us out of our apartment and were refusing to allow my mother to shop in their stores—the Quakers came and befriended us. They even escorted us to Ellis Island to make sure we were safe.

In 1942, we moved to Tokyo. We stayed with my aunt, my mother's oldest sister. We had lots of family in Japan—aunts and uncles and cousins. I went to an international school run by the Convent of the Sacred Heart and was taught by nuns. My brother and I could speak and understand Japanese, but we were terrible at reading and writing the language. Fortunately our instruction, at first, was in English.

Then the war got worse, and we weren't allowed to speak English: It was the enemy language. I stood out wherever I went because my clothes were so obviously American. We knew that people were watching us. We could go outside in the morning and find boot prints in the dirt: places where the secret police had stood near our windows at night, listening to what we were saying in the house.

Once again, friends from school were so important. But we had to be careful wherever we went. One day, a friend and I forgot and began speaking English on a public street. The principal called us into the office and said that we should never do that again! We were speaking the enemy language. It was dangerous.

As the war went on and the Americans got closer to Japan, there was first a campaign with incendiary bombs that was devastating to some Japanese cities, where the homes burned easily. At least during the firebombing, there was something we could do: we could join a bucket brigade to put out fires. I remember one woman stood up on her roof, sweeping cinders away with a broom.

But nothing could be done about these atomic bombs that could wipe out an entire city with a single blast. After the news of the first atomic bomb—and when the sirens went off again—we all went and sat in the air raid shelter, expecting to die right there.

Finally, the war ended and I was forced to choose a citizenship. If I chose to become Japanese, I would never see my American friends again. If I chose to become American, I would hurt my Japanese family members and friends. In the end, I chose to become an American because English was my language and the U.S. was the place where I had the greatest chance of completing my education and becoming independent.

I got a job working for the Allied Occupation of Japan, where I could earn money to pay for my passage back to the U.S. Then I enrolled at Radcliffe, and worked my way through college by looking after children for professors and other families.

What I remember most about the whole experience was the importance of friends, the surprise of these Quaker people who befriended us—and how doubly wonderful peace felt when the war was over!

Getting in touch with friends again after the war was absolute heaven!

The world seemed to begin again.

CHAPTER 23

Raj Chehl
Under the Acacia Tree

"Now my house is your home and your house is my home!"

Raj Chehl is a psychotherapist and founder of WiseLife, LLC. Additionally, Raj is a mom, yoga instructor, speaker, author, entrepreneur and co-host of the online radio show, "Living Life Powerfully." She is active in the interfaith community and has served on WISDOM's board. She also is a panelist on the Emmy award-winning television show, *Interfaith Odyssey*, representing her Sikh traditions. This successful life blossomed in spite of a childhood filled with major life transitions and adversity including war. Friendship, understanding and compassion served as an antidote in helping to heal the past and thrive in the present.

DEAFENING SIRENS WARNING of the impending danger of bombardment is something that no 6-year-old should have to endure—and yet I did during the 1965 Indo-Pakistani War. Shortly after sunset, friends and neighbors would gather at our home. Sleeping together under the canopy of stars on cots lined up in our veranda made it easier to reach the 8-foot-deep, Z-shaped trench which had been dug in our yard. Peak anxiety levels in anticipation of the mayhem that could unleash anytime in the darkness of the night was a daily occurrence. All too often, I remember being jolted out of my sleep as an adult would be scooping me up just before making a dash for the trench.

One beautiful afternoon, as I was playing outside, I heard the sirens blaring one after another. I immediately panicked and started screaming for Mom as I ran towards the trench. As I began to make my descent onto a flimsy chair placed in the trench for us little folks, the chair toppled and I came crashing down onto the muddy floor. I was wearing some glass bangles that shattered and were partially embedded in my right arm. Pain, fear, anger and confusion took over. I remember sitting in the trench just staring at my bloody arm, temporarily forgetting the sounds of war raging around me.

As my life flashed before me, a noise rose in my mind—a noise that grew even louder than the sirens. I could hear echoes of all the messages that I had picked up in my environment during my six years on this planet. Messages such as:

You can't trust any people from another country!

You are safe as long as you stick to your own religion!

You can't go to your friend's house because that family is different.

Strong, discriminating statements like these had embedded themselves in my thoughts, heightening my doubts and fears. They all bubbled up in this crazy moment of crisis where I had jumped into the trench and now sat there bleeding. Questions flooded my mind:

Why was someone bombing us?

Raj Chehl • 123

Did I do something wrong?
Are bad people pretending to be nice?
Can I ever trust a friend again?
Will my family be safe?

My own anxious thoughts—mingled with the shock and pain of my injury—stirred up that turbulent noise within my head. These experiences left me with an indescribable ambivalence toward our world.

When my family moved from India to the United States in 1966, we all committed ourselves to making a fresh start. Within a couple of months, I learned to speak English and before long, my peers accepted me. We played, talked, laughed and ate lunch together every day. My anxieties slowly began to subside as I experienced acceptance, respect, trust and love. I began to see that people from other faiths and cultures appear "different" only until you get to know them as people. Then we discover how much we share as human beings.

Then, in 1969, my family moved to Khartoum, Sudan, where my growing acceptance of diversity was tested in new ways. In Sudan, I was inundated with sights, sounds, people and places I had never experienced before—renewing the whirlwind of emotions and anxieties within me. The stress of acclimating once again drove me back to all the old questions and doubts that I experienced in the trench. Of course, I was a little older and a bit more mature. But, at the same time, I was even more sensitive to my surroundings and I was more self-conscious about the differences I perceived between myself and others around me.

My parents enrolled me in an Italian-Catholic school where I quickly learned to speak Italian and Arabic and once again made an effort to fit in. The endeavor paid off. Even though I was a Sikh girl from India, I befriended a Muslim girl from Pakistan, a Hindu girl from India and a Christian girl from Hungary. I do not know for sure if these new friends had similar doubts, fears and apprehensions, but I can tell you that my own subsided rapidly as we became more comfortable with each other. An amazing understanding and acceptance developed between us that transcended the tensions related to our differences in religion, race, creed, status and appearance.

We did not avoid our differences. In fact, the more we took an interest in each other's culture and religion, the more we found respect, acceptance and love growing between us.

Khartoum is one of the hottest major cities in the world with temperatures above 100 degrees beginning in April. There was a beautiful, sprawling acacia tree in a corner of the playground at our school and the shade felt like a gift from heaven in the sweltering heat. As soon as the recess bell rang, all four of us rushed to find our spots under the acacia tree.

One day I remember in particular, our Hungarian friend looked withdrawn, sad and sullen. I immediately asked, "Is everything OK?"

Tears began to flow uncontrollably down her cheeks as she explained what had happened the previous night. She told us that her grandmother was visiting the family. After my friend had gone into her bedroom for the night, she overheard her parents and grandmother having a conversation. She continued, "My grandmother told my parents that I should not be hanging around all of you!"

We were stunned! None of us understood why anyone would say such a thing. We sat dumbfounded in silence until another friend broke the silence. She asked, "Why?"

With hesitation for fear of hurting our feelings, she explained, "Grandma says that you will be a bad influence on me. She says that I need to be with children who are Christian and look like me." At this point, her tears were replaced with anger and she yelled out, "**I hate that! I hate what she said! I love all of you!**"

Teary-eyed, confused and sad for our dear friend, as if in a chorus we spoke in unison: "We love you!"

That day, that recess, that tree, that conversation, that love became deeply etched in all of us. Our friendship and love for each other grew stronger and even at this young age, we knew that we could not take our friendship for granted. We found practical solutions to her parents' new rules. Mainly, she was forbidden from visiting our homes—but we were not banned from her home. So, all of us availed ourselves of every opportunity to go to her house. It was always fun. When we would meet elsewhere, and our friend was absent, we would make sure that she felt included by calling her or writing nice letters to her.

The following year during recess time, we took shelter under the same beautiful tree. Our Hungarian friend was bursting at the seams with joy. There was pep in every step and with glistening eyes and an ear-to-ear smile, she announced that she had something to tell us.

What had happened? She had decided to open up to her parents about the conversation she had overheard with her grandmother. She said that her parents apologized to her and to all of us. They also acknowledged that her grandmother had a narrow worldview and was only trying to protect her only granddaughter from harm. And then the tears of joy streamed down her cheeks as she blurted out, "I have permission to come to *your* houses now!" None of us fully understood, until this moment, how confined she had.

Then she said something I will never forget. Her voice became soft, melodious and like a song being sung by the most beautiful bird—as if she was expressing something from her highest self. She said, "Now my house is your home and your house is my home!"

Our Sikh teachings emphasize the Oneness of God and the universal brotherhood and sisterhood of humankind. I am not sure if my dear Hungarian friend realized the profundity of her message but what I experienced that fine day still reverberates deeply in my heart.

Although we found ways to work around the barriers we had faced for a time, it was only when the unconditional love was allowed to flow unabated that all four of us felt the true joy and freedom of our sisterhood. No war, no sirens, no trench, no hate, no mistrust, no ambivalence and no fear—only understanding, acceptance, love, trust, reverence, freedom and universal Oneness.

CHAPTER 24

Jeanne Salerno
Souls in Dialogue

*"Out beyond ideas of wrongdoing and rightdoing,
there is a field. I'll meet you there."*

—Rumi

Jeanne Salerno is a social justice activist who has worked both professionally and on a personal level in southeast Michigan and in the Middle East and North Africa. While living in Egypt, Jeanne was inspired to build relationships and hold interreligious dialogue with Muslims who may not have otherwise known a Catholic Christian. This grassroots style of building interfaith relationships in Egypt is risky and yet Jeanne believes that this kind of connection is a deep yearning among countless souls around the world.

AS FAR BACK as elementary school, I remember daydreaming about life in faraway lands. When the classroom was quiet and other kids were busy working, I would imagine myself somewhere else experiencing life through other cultures. Though I was probably just 8 or 9, I would draw detailed pictures of places I visited in my daydreams to keep my memories alive. I sometimes wonder what my mother thought when her little girl brought home sketches of the Taj Mahal or the Great Pyramid of Giza. At a very early age, I remember feeling connected with something much larger, something that I longed for but could not grasp.

In 2005, an unexpected turn of events brought my dreams to life. While working as the vice president of retail banking and mortgage lending at a community-development bank in Detroit, I was offered a rare opportunity to co-author the *African Mortgage Toolkit*, a hands-on instruction manual for banks and non-bank financial institutions in Africa that wanted to begin mortgage lending. The tool kit was procured by the International Finance Corporation, which led to a contract with the United States Agency for International Development (USAID) to help establish a primary mortgage market in Egypt.

It was during this time that I was introduced to Seham, a knowledgeable Egyptologist who spoke perfect English. As I spent time with Seham touring Egypt, I realized that she was a very open-minded and welcoming person.

As an independent consultant to USAID and then to the World Bank Group, I spent several years in the Middle East and North Africa with a home base in Egypt. It was important to me that I lived not as an expatriate but as a local, in solidarity with Egyptians. Though I was a single American woman and a Catholic Christian, it never occurred to me that I would be treated any differently because of those factors. I lived in a unique community of 28 houseboats moored on the bank of the Nile. My once state-of-the-art boat had seen better days but it had weathered into an idealist's hideaway. Neighbors and friends were all eager to help me integrate into society and they were delighted to have an American lady who happened to be Christian in the neighborhood. I was a confidante to the women and taught English to the children. For people who were in the middle of a socioeconomic transition, my worldview may have seemed like a bona fide connection to the other side. Regardless of the practicalities, we met each other with a mutual embrace. I immediately felt a sense of belonging and took my place as a member of the community. At this point in time, I was beginning to sense the sacred space I would hold between cultures and religions. Very aware of that grace, I felt drawn to work for unity and peace through interreligious dialogue and began planning the way forward.

During the five-year span between 2005 and 2010, the Egyptian socioeconomic climate changed rapidly. But while the economic indicators were positive and the middle class was growing, nobody was measuring inequality or social justice. Egypt was heading toward a historic time of unrest. Fortuitously, I returned to America just prior to the Egyptian revolution of 2011 and remained in Michigan for three years. Through the Internet I was able to maintain relationships but I longed to be physically present in Egypt. My friend Seham knew this more than anyone.

Between 2011 and 2013, Egypt erupted with tumultuous events, including the overthrow of one president after another. During that period, I was in regular contact with Seham. Because security had become a threat for Egyptians, we often talked of the attributes of God as our hope for humanity. The fact that Seham is Muslim and I am Catholic made no difference. We were both completely comfortable drawing on wisdom, values and spiritual qualities from both religions. This had affirmed my sense that there is indeed a sacred energy in the space between religions. I was ready to return to Egypt. I also was very aware of the lingering discontent.

Divine timing is always perfect. In September 2014 I returned to Egypt to live with Seham and her family. When I sensed that the time was right for my work to begin, I went to an oasis with a friend who thought I might find some people interested in talking with me. While there is no law in Egypt against initiating interreligious dialogue, I knew that my grassroots type of interreligious dialogue was potentially dangerous because the motivation could be misunderstood as proselytizing Muslims. I took all this into consideration but decided that humanity would be far better off with people spreading the message of peace and unity than without these efforts.

We walked the dusty back roads until we reached a grassy oasis, which softened the sharp edge of the sunbaked Western Desert. As we came closer, I saw well-groomed Arabian horses roaming free in a flat green meadow surrounded by a thick band of brushy trees. Frilly white flowers bordered the edge of the tree line like lace trim. Near the center of the flat space stood a cluster of palm trees topped with tousled fronds that canopied a cozy sitting space where tea was served in china cups. When we first arrived, I noticed a family that appeared to be watching young children learn to ride the horses. Within a few minutes, several other people arrived and sat together under the canopy to escape the mid-afternoon heat. Then came more. Some exchanged greetings and spoke in Arabic. I wondered which of these people, if any, might be the ones who were interested in talking with me. To calm my jumbled thoughts, I walked away to pray, sensing something was about to happen.

When I returned from my short walk, my friend announced rather loudly that I was an American Christian living in Egypt who hoped to initiate dialogue between Muslims and Christians. Her voice carried and aroused the interest of others who were farther away. Within a few minutes, a group formed around me; they were all Muslim but all did not know one another. People were talking at once, asking who I was and why I was there. Humbly, I introduced myself and began to speak slowly because some in the group needed translation. "Dialogue" was not a familiar term to them and the moment I spoke the word, I knew that I needed to begin by defining dialogue in a religious context.

I spoke very few words after that. Each person wanted to share their personal story of a Muslim-Christian experience that had touched them very deeply. All of their stories shared a common theme of the separation between people because of their religious identity. Every story was told with hope and longing for a day when religious identity would not stand as a barrier to a soul's freedom to unite with others.

A few people recounted family stories of Muslim-Christian connections that went back as far as their ancestors; how they lived as neighbors and ate meals together, how they regularly read sacred Scripture together from the Bible and Qur'an and how they praised one God. One man spoke about scholarly interreligious work that had been published by a family member but now was out of print. A woman expressed her innermost desire to establish an organization that would teach children the value of religious diversity, peacemaking and unity. Every now and then, when something prompted us, we acknowledged the correlation between the truth in our stories and Scripture in our holy books.

Throughout the exchange, we welcomed our tears as a precious gift and consoled one another when grief was too heavy to bear. And when we came to the end of our journey together that sacred afternoon, we held one another. As the sun dipped into the desert horizon and it was time to part, we knew that, through the sharing of our souls that afternoon, we had participated in the fulfillment of our own stories.

As my circle of friends grew over time, it was evident that our connection was unique and the way we had chosen to live in our sacred space demonstrated the joy and gratitude of souls free to love one another without any limitations. Whether I was in Egypt, Palestine, Yemen or elsewhere, my experience had repeatedly been the same: that souls were longing to connect, with or without words, even if only for a fleeting moment. People want to share stories, to listen and be heard, and at the end of the day, discover themselves through one another. Participating in this process inspired me to create space for other people to experience this integral type of human fulfillment. I feel strongly that the souls of all individuals are conjoined and we, as human beings, can fulfill our highest purpose when we understand that we have a share in one another and revere that connection as sacred.

Today, violence in Egypt has flared up against Christians in a calculated effort by extremists to destabilize the country. This terrorist activity is in contrast with what I have learned from my interaction with both Muslim and Christian Egyptians. In a country where more than 90 percent of the people identify with the Muslim faith, I feel certain that most Egyptians desire a unified and peaceful society; many Muslims are reaching out to protect Coptic (Egyptian) Christians and others are consistently praying for their safety. Both Muslim and Coptic clerics pray for peace. God willing, I will return to my home in Cairo with Seham, whom I love dearly and call "my sister." And I shall humbly take my place, in solidarity with Egyptians, to bring Christian and Muslim souls together for the sake of unity and peace.

Through this long journey, I have found comfort in the poetry of the 13th-century Muslim mystic and poet known as Rumi. I particularly love his poem *Out Beyond Ideas*:

Out beyond ideas of wrongdoing and rightdoing,

there is a field. I'll meet you there.

When the soul lies down in that grass,

the world is too full to talk about.

Ideas, language, even the phrase "each other"

doesn't make any sense.

CHAPTER 25

Blair and Beverly Nichols
A Friendship That Circled the World

*"I have something for you,"
Barbara said. And that
heightened my suspicions.
Was this one last attempt
to save our souls?*

As representatives of their Baháʼí
faith, Blair and her mother, Beverly
Nichols, devoted years of their lives
to re-establishing historic links to a
Native American community. They
discovered more friction than they
expected, not from Native Americans, but from other outsiders
trying to work with the Indian families. Blair writes their story.

IN 1979, MY young son, Shariff, and I moved from inner-city Detroit to the Omaha Indian Reservation in Macy, a small town in northeast Nebraska. The town was established in 1906 and its name is a compound of syllables from the original name for this location: the U.S. Omaha Agency. Macy also holds a special place in Bahá'í history as the first all-Indian Bahá'í Spiritual Assembly in the world, established in 1947. Our faith teaches us to value diversity in our communities; and Bahá'ís took great pride when this Omaha tribe chose to join us in honoring the oneness of humanity through Baha'u'llah's teachings.

We arrived on January 9, 1979, in the midst of what we were told was the coldest winter in 30 years. At the same time, we learned that a Dutch Reformed minister's family also had moved to Macy to work with the Indians.

Our initial contact was Steve Walker, a Bahá'í who encouraged his mother, Zollie Walker, to rent her empty one-room house to us. Years ago, Zollie had raised her children in that home, even though it had only rudimentary utilities—electricity, a wood stove for heating and propane for cooking. Our water came from an outside cold-water faucet. Instead of a bathroom, we had an outhouse. Overall, I was thankful to find a place among the Omaha people. Our home was a stone's throw from the elementary school.

The only woman who came to introduce herself was Barbara, who was white. Until her visit, I had not felt like a strange addition to Macy, but Barbara burst into my home full of nosy questions, making it clear to me that she found it odd to meet a single black woman with a child moving into the community. As our first meeting unfolded, I learned that Barbara was a Dutch Reformed missionary. She zeroed in on Shariff and asked me lots of questions like: "Is he safe? Will he be adequately provided for?"

In my eyes, Barbara was odd. Until our move to Macy, I had lived my entire life in the black community. As she was pressing me with her questions, I was thinking: *Who is this loud, white woman demanding answers to her questions as if someone had placed her in charge of my family?* I certainly did not feel friendly toward her.

Nevertheless, I began to tell her my story: I felt honored to help restore our historic Bahá'í Spiritual Assembly. But, Barbara was not interested. She looked at me in total disbelief. I was a missionary, too? She had never heard of the Bahá'í faith, but told me that I was "from a competing religion" trying to reach *her* beloved Omaha people. She seemed to assume she already owned some religious right to this indigenous community. I was happy to see her leave my house. Of course, Macy was so small that I soon realized I would be running into her, her husband and her gregarious children everywhere I went in the community.

After only a few months of living in Macy, I invited my mother, who also is Bahá'í, to join us and help with Shariff, who was 4, and with my efforts to restore a Bahá'í community. We also welcomed my younger brother Brett who was just entering high school.

Immediately, Brett encountered Barbara's children at school and the kids hit it off. Barbara's children regarded Brett as a friendly teddy bear from Detroit, an impression heightened when Brett became our local school's best hope for a better football season. Barbara welcomed Brett into her family. After all, Brett made it clear that he did not consider himself a Bahá'í and was not interested in converting anyone.

That was another misunderstanding. I was not planning to convert Omaha tribal members. I was there to locate any remaining members of families who had been active in 1947. As I got to know people, though, I realized that most Omahas felt connected to the Native American Church, where they could use their own language, singing, drumming, pipes and had ceremonies for healing, for marking the seasons and for celebrating life-cycle events. They had a ritual for the dead that included singing prayers and drumming throughout the night. I still recall hearing that music at 4 a.m. Not every member of the tribe was an active member of the Church, but nearly everyone in the community felt it was their first spiritual affiliation—and anything else came after that. They had a deep respect for religion, believing that all faiths came from one God. So, they welcomed both Barbara's and my family to live among them. From the Omahas, I learned not to criticize other religious traditions. They would have considered such aggressive activity truly strange. I made up my mind to get along with the competing groups in this very small town.

Brett began to spend all of his time while not at school and football practice at Barbara's house. He ate there, watched TV and enjoyed the company of the other children. Then he would come home to sleep at our house. I did not admit it at the time, but I was pleased at first. I was working and going to school myself. Sometimes, Brett would take Shariff with him to Barbara's home. When he did that, I knew Shariff had a safe, warm place to spend time when I was not at home. Nevertheless, I remained very concerned that Barbara wanted, on her terms, "to save souls." And, sure enough, Shariff came home one day and asked if I was saved. Then, he told me that Barbara had made sure that his soul was saved. It seemed to me as though little Shariff had fallen under Barbara's spell.

I was furious! She had crossed the line. How dare she teach religion to my son! Brett was older and could hold his own. But to go after Shariff? I wanted to march over to Barbara's house and confront her! I told Shariff his days at Barbara's house were over. I was going to set new limits: No more tagging along with Brett and spending long afternoons with Barbara's kids. Of course, I also explained to him that he already was "saved"—and not because of anything Barbara had told him. I said, "God loves all of us and we are all saved."

That was the start of the silent war between Barbara and me. I would see her on many occasions, including football games and community funerals. Often, I would glare at her with real resentment in my heart for telling my son that we were not saved. Brett continued to spend time at her home. But there was no war between my mother and Barbara. Beverly was extremely grateful to her for being there for Brett until she was able to arrive in Macy months later and resume providing Brett with a home so that he could thrive. Beverly always felt warmth and understanding toward Barbara and easily forgave her for talking to Shariff about being "saved."

Time passed. Brett grew up and graduated with the offer of a four-year football scholarship at a small college. Barbara's six children grew up and went off to college. Fifteen years later, in 1994, my mother and I began to make plans to leave Macy to teach English in China. We both were happy to associate with the Chinese people and learn a new culture. Formal missionary work was forbidden in China, but we knew we could share an awareness of our spirituality through our daily presence with our students. The news spread through Macy about our move to Asia.

Although we were pleased at this new prospect, my mother began to have trouble sleeping because of her anxiety about the long list of hurdles we had to clear before the trip—passports, visas, shots and so many other arrangements for our new life in China. As I talked with her about these mounting anxieties, I was thunderstruck to learn her biggest fear: Our clothes were shabby! After years of our routines in Macy, we had fallen into wearing a limited number of comfortable clothes that fit our daily work. My mother had been working as a nurse and had a nurse's uniform. We were about to leave Macy with only a handful of well-worn clothes between us. Mother insisted that we would make a poor impression in our new Chinese home. Unfortunately, I had no idea how to allay her fears. We had always lived on a very limited budget. There was no money for shopping.

My solution was encouraging my mother to write a letter to God. I said, "Get out a piece of paper and start with: Dear God, we need ... " and she did just that! Her beautiful face lit up as she began to write. If nothing else, that letter-writing project gave her some peace and relieved my own anxieties about her adjustment to our big move. Eventually, she finished her letter and I urged her to place it under her pillow as an expression of her prayerful yearning.

Our spirits, once again, rose as we anticipated our journey and I ticked off the final items on our long list of preparations. Then, on one of our last days, my mother and I went to the post office and ran into Barbara. We looked at each other sternly, as we always did, but then Barbara surprised me with an invitation to her home. Brett and Shariff had spent countless hours at her home, but my mother and I had never received such an invitation. Naturally, I was suspicious.

"I have something for you," Barbara said. And that heightened my suspicions. Was this one last attempt to save our souls? I didn't want to go get whatever was waiting for us in her house.

That's when my mother warmly smiled and told Barbara that we would come. Now we were committed. When we walked into Barbara's home, both of us were surprised to find two brand new suitcases! I was shocked. My surprise grew when Barbara opened the cases and we realized they were filled with new clothes. They were even in our sizes! Mother's prayerful list in her letter to God was realized before us—from knee-high stockings to London Fog raincoats. I'm sure that Barbara had never seen the actual letter, but somehow the intention had resonated with her own heart. We were speechless. There were no words to describe our wonderment at what was unfolding before our eyes.

Barbara confessed to us that she loved shopping and bought new clothes with any extra money she had—too many clothes. In fact, she bought so many things, she told us, that she had clothing in storage that she had never worn. When she heard we were heading to China, her over abundance of clothes led her to think of this gift. But not before she faced her own anxieties, she told us. Her own missionary zeal prevented her from doing anything that might help us to teach the Bahá'í faith. So, Barbara prayed and struggled with her decision to give us the clothes. God finally reassured her that it was a good thing to provide this gift.

The whole time we were in China, we wore Barbara's clothes. We even encountered more evangelical missionaries like Barbara, who had come to China as English teachers and were trying to touch the lives of their students. For Barbara's sake, we were kind to them, even when those missionaries met us with obvious bias. Remembering Barbara, I would hold my tongue and try to greet them in sincere love and charity. That approach to hospitality lies at the heart of our own Bahá'í tradition. Baha'u'llah taught: "Do not be content with showing friendship in words alone, let your heart burn with loving kindness for all who may cross your path."

In 1994, when we went to China, Barbara had been diagnosed with breast cancer. In 1997 we visited Macy again and attended a funeral. As we sat down in the congregation, we saw Barbara just entering. She knew nearly everyone in attendance but, that day, she chose to sit with us. As we greeted each other, she whispered that she still had breast cancer and did not know the outcome. She asked us: "Will you girls keep me in your prayers?"

Later, when we were in South America we heard that Barbara had died. My mother and I joined in a quiet prayer for the departed. In this case, our prayers were for a woman who had become our friend, and who we knew loved her Lord. Her act of submission in deciding to make a generous gift to us had opened our hearts to love her. She could have kept her clothing to herself, but she admitted to us that she felt God leading her to make this gift. As she experienced that change of heart and then showed such generosity to us, our hearts were opened to appreciate others from her evangelical background, even when we encountered hostility from them.

Now, when I think of Barbara, my eyes fill with tears and I say: "God bless her."

CHAPTER 26

Judith Anne Satterthwaite
Melting the Cold War

*The beauty of the times we had just shared
made her startling revelation a minor piece
of who she had become in my eyes.*

"Judy" is an industrial consultant living in southeast Michigan. As a child, she was raised a Christian Scientist, which she says helped her focus on the positive aspects of life—and of the people she meets. Growing up in a religious minority also gave her an appreciation for others who are in the minority. Judy believes that being different can be good if one is willing to accept and love oneself, and others, as cherished children of God. Although she eventually left the Christian Science Church, Judy believes that the foundation of unconditional love has greatly influenced her life.

ABOUT 20 YEARS ago, a Russian professor from Kiev named Valerie Kadyrov contacted me and asked if I would be interested in selling his product in the United States. Having been in sales for a while, I already knew that I loved to converse and mingle with others. I told him that I would be more than happy to help sell his product.

I ended up visiting Kiev, Ukraine, in December 1991. I wanted to see the product I would be selling—which was, in fact, a detonation coating process—in operation, so that I could better explain and sell the idea to customers in the U.S. I also brought a cash advance from another partner in the U.S. so that the Kadyrov family would have some money to work with.

My visit occurred just after the Soviet Union was dissolved, and it was quite apparent that the economy was struggling. I stayed with Valerie Kadyrov and his wife Ludmila in their apartment. Valerie's son Erik was studying advanced physics at the University of Wisconsin and was hoping to work on a superconductor. When I arrived in Kiev, their daughter moved in with a friend temporarily so that I could stay in her room.

Professor Kadyrov was one of the 5,000 Ph.D.s working at the Institute of Materials Sciences in Kiev—he was part of the Russian "brain trust" living in that city. At the collapse of the Soviet Union, the institute had no money. As a result, many of the scientists who had "sale-able" projects were trying to market them in whatever way they could. There were many other technical advances developed at the institute in addition to the coating process that Valerie was trying to market to the U.S. During a tour of the facilities, I saw a fabric of Basalt rock, made by melting the rock and forming it into a fine hollow thread that was then woven into a silky fabric. There was a demonstration of new welding processes—glass to metal (very new at the time)—and several other advances in materials applications.

The Kadyrov home was a modest, two-bedroom apartment. The hallways were dark and we always walked up the stairs to their floor because electricity was at a premium. They had put up and decorated a small Christmas tree for me in their sitting room. During the course of my visit, Ludmila took me to see the art museum, a beautiful church, and displays of miniatures and historical artifacts. At the museum, the lights were turned on when visitors entered a room and quickly turned off as soon as they moved on. Heat was kept at a minimum. I was especially intrigued by the fact that Ukraine had new currency—but no coins! As a result, all the pay phones in the city were free. People were expected to "take turns" using the phones so all could make their calls as needed. Ludmila was determined that I see the beauty and culture of Kiev, while Valerie insisted I visit the war museum, which was fronted by a statue that paid tribute to victory and Russian MiG planes.

Both of the Kadyrovs were very concerned for my safety. I was never to go out alone! Even when I ventured out with Ludmila, Valerie suggested that I wear one of her coats so I didn't look so "Western." I would spend evenings telling Ludmila about my sons and my life in America. She understood more English than I did Russian. I learned how to say "okay" in Russian—we both said that word a lot!

Ludmila and Valerie were also intent upon showing me a pleasant time, so we ate at an ice cream parlor and went to a circus. Valerie's daughter and her boyfriend took me to see a performance of *Romeo and Juliet* by the Russian Ballet Theater at the Kiev Opera House. Money and goods were **very** scarce, so I appreciated all they did to make me feel welcome.

The last evening, Ludmila and I shopped for groceries. She struggled mightily with a decision to buy (or not buy) a cake for dessert. In the end, she left me at the car and ran back to the bakery to get the cake for my last dinner with them. I expressed my wonder, which bordered on awe, at all that she was able to do to care for her family under such difficult circumstances. That's when she told me that she was used to hardships and difficulties—years before, when her children were small, they lived in a secure village in the Ural Mountains where she had worked as a nuclear scientist. In fact, she had traveled to Cuba and other countries around the world, to help with the installation of nuclear weapons facilities for the Communist government! I was, at first, both surprised and stunned. However, the beauty of the times we had just shared made her startling revelation a minor piece of who she had become in my eyes. She was Ludmila, the gentle soul who was a gracious hostess under difficult circumstances, who laughed with me and cried with me, and struggled to speak some English to me when I could speak very little Russian.

The sweet little blond woman who had opened her home and her heart to me was one of the Russian nuclear scientists that we, in the West, had pictured as demonic monsters! She was no monster—she was a loving wife to her husband, a mom who worried about her kids and someone who had welcomed a visitor from the United States into her home, demonstrating a truly warm heart.

If we are willing to be open to others—to listen and learn and share—we will find many more similarities than differences. Even though languages and circumstances may separate us, hearts can unite us.

CHAPTER 27

Shari Rogers
Opening Doors, Opening Eyes, Opening Hearts

Together, we can create unity in place of isolation; trust in place of fear; and love in place of misunderstanding.

Shari is a psychologist who is active in Jewish organizations and, now in her 40s, is devoting more time to studying the religious teachings and traditions of Judaism. Through religious study, her larger assumptions about the world are expanding. Specifically, her study of Torah has enhanced both her understanding of herself and of all relationships. One of her first interreligious encounters enlarged her awareness in a surprising way.

I GREW UP in a home where intellectual life and appreciation of all cultures was celebrated. My parents were both Master's-level Bridge players who enjoyed Bridge three nights a week with people from many different backgrounds. They were very open in the friendships they formed, as well as in their intellectual interests. Our family traveled extensively around the world, thus giving me a comfort level with all people.

My education in Judaism began at Jewish Day School and culminated sadly with my Bat Mitzvah. But it was my sister Darra's increasing religious observance during adulthood that sparked my interest in learning both the Torah and the Jewish studies that I have pursued during the past decade. In addition, I received my doctorate in clinical psychology, where I was trained in the psychoanalytic model. As much as I respect using psychoanalytic principles in helping other people to achieve personal growth, they have their limitations. I believe that the tenets of Judaism have at least as much—if not more—potential to enhance a person's life.

I remember visiting the Holocaust museum in Jerusalem. One particular insight from my guide remains with me to this day: He said that intellect alone—without a heart and soul, without a moral center to our lives—is not enough in this world. He pointed out that in the 1930s, many of the people who joined the Nazi party were very well-educated and culturally-sophisticated people—doctors, artists, musicians and educators—and they still fell under the spell of Hitler's words. As the guide spoke of his experiences that day, it became clear to me that the vast intellectual and scientific accomplishments the world has seen in the last few decades will not serve as a deterrent to injustice, hatred and intolerance.

In my recent studies of Judaism , I have come to understand why one of the most important tenets is *Tikkun Olam* (rectification of the world) because the Torah recognizes that every human being has to battle to overcome negative character traits within him- or herself. Every person has a destructive potential within. Therefore, the goal is to first recognize this, and to engage in a struggle with self, and then to use free will to change this negative potential. The outcome of this struggle will help the individual to be kinder in thoughts, words and actions, and the world becomes a better place. If we fail to do this and if we let our nature control us, it becomes possible for the brightest and most cultured individuals to perpetrate the worst crimes in the history of humanity

My friend, Brenda Rosenberg, is very involved in interfaith groups like WISDOM and in projects like Reuniting the Children of Abraham. She is always trying to bring people together, across their individual boundary lines. When she knew that I was getting more deeply involved in religious studies, she invited me to go with her to an international conference called "ENGAGING the OTHER" that was held at Oakland University. I found it fascinating to meet so many people—especially Muslim clerics and Arab community leaders from as far away as Saudi Arabia—who were willing to be in a space that focused on creating understanding.

Next, Brenda invited me to visit a mosque; her friend, Hind Kabawat, a peace activist from Syria, flew in to be part of the program. This was a mosque that most Jews never visit. We knew that a large crowd was expected, but were shocked to find that 900 people were in attendance. I must admit, I was apprehensive. I questioned whether or not I should really be in a mosque. Was I betraying my faith? Some of my other friends voiced their concerns. They told me I was absolutely insane for doing this. They were afraid for my safety.

We walked into this mosque, covering our heads with scarves in respect for the Muslims' traditions. This wasn't awkward for me. I am aware of the importance of covering one's head to communicate modesty. My sister is an observant Jew who dresses modestly and covers her hair. I was touched by the similarity.

We were warmly greeted. Brenda knew so many people, and you could sense that, with these people, she had real friendships; she even received hugs from most of the women.

As we were ushered to a front table, next to the key dignitaries and speakers, a woman sitting next to me leaned over and said: "You look very familiar to me!"

I thought: What is she thinking? She must be mistaking me for someone else.

Then she said, "Oh, I know you!"

I knew that wasn't possible.

When she mentioned my parents' names, I was flabbergasted. This woman in a mosque knows my parents' names? How could she know?

"Through Bridge," she continued. "We were friends with your parents. Are they still playing Bridge?"

I sat there, stunned. But she was already inquiring about the welfare of my various family members. Suddenly here I was, in the middle of this mosque, catching up on all the latest family news with this Muslim woman.

The experience was eye-opening. My fears and the fears of my friends had sullied what I had prided myself on most: being an open, empathic person who likes to connect to people.

This woman's connection to my family members shattered the glass that seemed to separate us. We had so much more in common than our appearances might suggest, and even more to share and give if we could only reach through that new opening between us.

In times when religion and cultural values are distorted to justify hatred and dissension, wouldn't it be amazing if, instead, we could open new doors to kindness and love of humanity? Together, we can create unity in place of isolation, trust in place of fear, and love in place of misunderstanding. If each person does what they can to open doors, we will surely see *Tikkun Olam*—a world repaired, a world at peace.

CHAPTER 28

Sheri Schiff
When People Change

*He had a fit, an absolute fit. ... My
boss said I had deceived him.*

By training, Sheri is an educator.
By nature, she's always been a
front-line, first-person advocate
for equality and opportunity
for all. She's trained others in
anti-bias and multi-cultural
education. Sheri is a leader in
her Jewish community, a docent
for the Holocaust Memorial

Center in Farmington Hills, Michigan, and a member of
outreach groups such as WISDOM. Because of her compassion,
courage and convictions, she has built personal connections
across racial, cultural and religious boundaries.

I CANNOT REMEMBER the first time I met a person from another race or religion or ethnic group because I grew up in a fairly diverse neighborhood in Detroit. My childhood friends were Italian, African-American and Jewish. But there were so many rules in each family; in my family, I could not make friends unless they were high achievers in school.

I am a second-generation American who grew up in an observant Jewish home. My grandparents came to this country fleeing pogroms in Russia. After my parents divorced—when I was around 3—my grandmother raised me while my mother went to work. I lived with my grandmother, mother, aunt and uncle and spent lots of time with my great-aunts and great-uncles, as well as my great-grandmother—my *bubbe*.

Everyone in the neighborhood knew a little Yiddish, a little Italian and some of the black-American colloquialisms. Both my grandmother and our African-American neighbors raised chickens in our backyards. We exchanged chicken recipes, but not the food: Ours were slaughtered kosher. I ate only kosher food or kosher-style food.

I jumped double-dutch with the girl next door, but was not allowed to eat in her house—although she always ate in ours. Her mom kept cookies with a *Cheksher*—a kosher seal—in the house, so that I could have a snack there.

I was allowed to go to my black neighbor's church, but not the Italian neighbor's Catholic church.

I was told, as a child, that if I had a problem or needed help that I should ask a black person. My family trusted our Italian neighbors, but made sure that I stayed out of their Catholic churches because they were afraid that I would be seized by the church and baptized against my will. Their paranoia was due to the difficulties they had experienced as Jews in Russia and as immigrants when they came to America.

I was arrested for civil rights protests for the first time when I was 15. There was a segregated swimming pool in Detroit: the Crystal Pool off of 8 Mile Road between Greenfield and Schaefer roads. I was arrested, and my grandmother and uncle bailed me out of jail. I remember my Grandmother Rose speaking Yiddish to the judge—who understood her telling him she wouldn't punish me for standing up to discrimination.

My personal hero is my Grandmother Rose—may she rest in peace. Rose Kallman Bakst was a courageous woman who walked out of Eastern Europe, made peace with a brutal situation, survived a pogrom and lived her life with dignity and grace. She was not schooled, but was fluent in English, Yiddish, Russian and Polish—all spoken with an Eastern European accent. She stood up to injustice and taught me the saying that I live by: "Justice, justice, you shall pursue."

When I was at Michigan State University for my graduate assistantship in the Department of Communications, I worked in the cooperative extension service doing drug-education work. My boss thought I was Italian, because my last name was Terebelo: That name reflected my adopted father's family, which was Italian Jewish.

My boss invited me to his home for dinner one night. There I was, at the dinner table, and I looked down at my plate; the main course that night was ham.

I took one look at the ham and said to myself : I'm not going to break *kashrut*—Hebrew for kosher—for him.

You know when you sometimes shove food around your plate to make it look like you're eating? That's what I was doing. Well, his mother-in-law—who made the ham—noticed I wasn't eating. My boss noticed too, and I said that I wasn't really hungry, but he would not let it go.

Finally, I told him it wasn't part of my diet, that I was Jewish and that I kept kosher.

He had a fit, an absolute fit. His mother started talking about fumigating the chairs. His kids started talking about Jews killing Jesus. My boss said I had deceived him.

After that, I had a tough time at work. My boss assigned me out of the office to Howell High School, when that area of Michigan was known for being home to local leaders of the Ku Klux Klan. I came into my office one day and there was a noose in there. Once, as I was driving in the area, I thought I was headed into a nice sunset—and soon realized it was a burning cross.

That was my trial by fire, surviving my work there.

But the story doesn't end there. In the early 1990s, one young man prompted change. He was a graduate of the Howell Public School District who went off to the University of Michigan where he found that his randomly assigned roommate was African-American. This roommate was a graduate of one of the Detroit area's most rigorous prep schools, but the Howell graduate was enraged at the living situation. He failed in an attempt to get another roommate and, instead, divided the room with a piece of tape. But one night, when the white student was stuck over a math problem, his black roommate offered advice on how to get the answer. The white student begrudgingly thanked him. The line down the middle of the room faded a bit. Another night, the black student invited his roommate to have dinner with his buddies. Little by little, the white student found his racist beliefs shattered simply by getting to know his roommate.

This white student carried that personal transformation further. He went back to his old school and demanded that administrators and teachers change. They agreed to try to start teaching differently. And, that has prompted my own reconnection with these schools. I was invited to facilitate workshops and help revise teaching materials. Twenty years had passed since my first encounters in Howell, but I was witnessing that change is possible even in such tough situations.

I know how complex it can be to navigate relationships in a diverse world. I've lived with these issues all my life. But I've also taught people how to make the changes that can welcome a more diverse society.

Entire communities can change—but it takes people to spark that transformation.

CHAPTER 29

The Rev. Sharon Buttry
From Conflict in the Streets to Healing Waters

The biggest surprise for me in this very difficult experience was how much there is in common among the Abrahamic traditions.

The Rev. Sharon is a Baptist pastor who works in cross-cultural urban ministry. Her ministry ranges from working with educational groups to leading retreats to activating peace in a way that trains and empowers society's most vulnerable people.

I DON'T THINK of the Kingdom of God in the hereafter. I think of it as something that is possible now.

In Ezekiel, we have the biblical image of the healing of nations that begins with water flowing from the sanctuary of God, spreading out across the land, bringing its healing power to all it touches. The work that I do—advocating for and teaching self-advocacy to those who are disenfranchised within their own communities—often feels like rowing against the stream. It can be very challenging to bring people together to work in a common direction. It's difficult to change a culture of conflict in which people define themselves by their differences, rather than by their common human experiences. But then there are other times when it all comes together in fellowship; you can almost feel the current of a community united around truth and a cause carrying you forward.

I like to say that I was born in a cornfield east of Columbus, Ohio, and grew up in farmland. I wasn't really born in a field, of course, but it was an isolated, rural area and such a contrast to the asphalt and concrete that surrounds my home these days. As I grew up, my Protestant family was very involved in the church. My dad was a lay preacher—not theologically trained—but the church was the center of our lives. Every Saturday, it seemed, we cleaned the church, and when we weren't doing that, we were there doing other activities. My mother was very service-oriented as well, visiting the sick and writing letters for the blind in nursing homes. In our church, 13 was the age of accountability, and I went through a passage of baptism, making a serious commitment to faith at that time in my life.

I was 19 when I married my husband. He was the son of an American Baptist Air Force chaplain and we decided that our purpose as a couple was to put God first in our lives. He went to seminary and became a pastor and is now working in international peace and justice work. I earned an M. Div, too—the master's degree that prepares clergy for ministry—and I also earned a master's in social work, so today I am both an American Baptist pastor and a Licensed Master Social Worker. That training equipped me to fully join my husband in dedicating our lives to serving others and in bringing about peace and justice. For us it is centered in Christian theology—Jesus laid down His life in love for people, and that's a model we take very seriously. He taught love of one's enemies, which is a unique teaching—the idea that you can embrace and clothe and feed your enemy. Reconciliation is a very powerful force in our theology. It's been a wonderful journey.

My job brought us to the Detroit area. My goal was to work in disenfranchised communities. From 1996–2005, I directed a nonprofit social service center for the American Baptist Church, and then, in 2005, I partnered with Pastor John Myers, who started ACTS 29 Fellowship. In this new work, our model was to meet physical, emotional and social needs; that's the kind of work I was doing the first nine years. But in ACTS 29, we now also pay close attention to spiritual needs and provide opportunities for spiritual growth for all ages in a worshipping community.

The Fellowship has grown out of the people who've been touched by the ministries: We now have a construction team that does home repair; we teach English as a second language; we reach out to kids through summer camping and backpacking, in Michigan and in other states. Each time we grow I think of Ezekiel and those waters flowing from the Sanctuary of God, bringing healing to the nations.

There are rough waters, too, in this kind of work! In 2004, we faced a major problem in Hamtramck, the small city where I work, and where there is a large Muslim population living among a shrinking Polish-Catholic population. One of the growing mosques wanted to broadcast its call to prayer over loudspeakers to the surrounding neighborhood, much like mosques do in Muslim communities around the world. Leaders of this mosque asked the City Council for guidance on moving forward in a way that would be in keeping with local ordinances. The City Council reviewed the sound ordinance and realized that an amendment would be required that would recognize this kind of outdoor use of loudspeakers for congregations. This became a much larger issue, because it turned out that local Catholic churches had been broadcasting musical calls to prayer that were in violation of the existing ordinance. The amendment essentially would have permitted all the houses of worship do this. Working with the imam to try to resolve this problem was my first interfaith experience as an adult.

Some people rose up against the idea of allowing a mosque to make its public call to prayer. In fact, some opposition groups came into Hamtramck from other parts of the country to protest. Before the issue was resolved, news reporters came from all over the world, and some confrontations were tense—especially in the streets with some of the protest groups.

I worked with a group of Muslim and Christian leaders who simply pointed out that these religious expressions from congregations were consistent with the Constitution. We tried to dispel stereotypes. We wove new interfaith partnerships. We began a Hamtramck interfaith clergy group, which included Jewish participation as well.

The biggest surprise for me in this very difficult experience was how much there is in common among the Abrahamic traditions: Judaism, Christianity and Islam.

In this case, we were working specifically with Christians and Muslims, and it was fun for me to help people from many different backgrounds see that these two faiths that seemed to be at odds actually share important truths that we believe make a difference beyond this life. The imam and I were very open about our traditions' propensities to proselytize and, once that was out in the open, we could say: "I know I am not going to convert you, but we still can be friends and find common ground and plenty of things to do together to make our community a more upright place."

How wonderful it would sound if that was the end of my story, with hands clasped across differences. But this is truly the story of a flow of water—a river of relationships that keeps flowing and changing. Sometimes, we don't agree on where this water should be taking us.

In 2008, religious groups once again got involved in a local political struggle. This time, the confrontation involved a proposed human rights ordinance in an effort to broadly prohibit discrimination in housing, employment and public accommodations; and this time, the ordinance included sexual orientation. New attitudes surfaced, including the biases of some outsiders who came into our town and challenged the ordinance. Opponents of these proposed civil-rights protections gathered enough signatures to place the proposed ordinance on a local ballot, assuming they could defeat the idea this way.

My husband and I worked tirelessly to promote the idea that all people deserve the chance to live and work where they want, even if their sexual orientation is different from our own.

This time around, our good friends in the Muslim community took up an opposing position on the ballot. It broke our hearts to hear the things people said against their neighbors. As happened with my earlier work on protecting the call to prayer, I met a whole new group of people in my community; we had never crossed paths until this new effort arose in our community.

As I worked to build support for the ordinance, my friend the imam called me and—this time—he raked me over the coals for supporting the ordinance. In this case, the ballot initiative failed and the human-rights ordinance was lost.

But, my friendship with the imam remains, I hope. We have met since the ballot initiative. I don't believe that our relationship, forged in the heat of community activism in support of Muslim neighbors, was just utilitarian on his part. It was genuine and I hope we will get back to working together again.

Part of what fuels my hope is the vision of our community, someday, as a jewel of diversity and peace—the kind of community where others will want to live, as well. But the only way to make that vision a reality is by working through our faith traditions. We need to transform character in the very places where character has become destructive and violent in its expression.

The healing waters described in Ezekiel have no end because they flow from God's sanctuary. The waters, like God's love, are endless. That's what gives me hope. That's what keeps me working to bring God's Kingdom to the here and now.

CHAPTER 30

Jatinder Kaur
A Heaven on Earth—
If We All Work Together

*In a civilized society, who dares to make fun
of a person on the threshold of his home?*

Jatinder Kaur came to the
United States from India in 1996
with her husband and two sons.
Volunteering and working at
her children's schools led to her
position of teaching English as a
second language in the Macomb
Intermediate School District
(MISD). In addition, she has
helped to advance the cause of
adult literacy through volunteer
positions at Macomb Literacy
Partners and the Sikh Society of
Michigan.

IN THE 1990s, friends encouraged me to move from my home in Punjab in northern India to the United States. They said things like: "You are lucky to have a chance to go." "You must go!" "You can expect a happy and peaceful life there." "All good things await you there." Some friends actually told me: "America is heaven on earth."

I was reluctant. I could read and write in English, but speaking it was a challenge. My husband was eager to move, because his whole family already lived in the U.S. We arrived in the U.S. in early 1996 to start our new life.

I expected challenges, but not the kind of heartbreaking confrontations we faced. In India, I was used to living in a diverse democratic country. I expected the U.S. would be the same—but I soon found it was not. We are Sikhs and, because of our distinctive dress, people stared at us with strange expressions. Some mistook our sons for girls because of their long hair. I encountered hostility from strangers here that I had never experienced in India.

More than once, I told my husband, "Let's go back."

One traumatic incident happened just two weeks after my arrival. My father-in-law was driving my two young sons, my sister-in-law and me on a freeway in southeast Michigan. We were chatting about our family and enjoying the ride. Suddenly, some people in another car opened their windows and started yelling, **"Go back to your country, you ... "** and they used bad words as they waved their fingers at us. We tried to ignore them, but they were very aggressive. They drove parallel with us, then in front of us, behind us—constantly shifting positions and yelling at us the whole time. My sister-in-law suggested heading directly to a police station, rather than continuing to our home. By the time we reached the police, the abusive drivers had veered away, but I was shivering with fear. We reported the incident but, because we had not made note of the license plate number of the car, the police never caught anyone.

After that, I thought: If this is America—we definitely should leave. I was confused, hurt and angry.

Unfortunately, that was not the only anti-immigrant incident. When my older son was in the fifth grade and my younger one was in kindergarten, they were both growing out their hair following Sikh tradition (our sons used to wear small turbans, eventually they would wear turbans like my husband). One day, when I reached school to pick up my boys, I was horrified to find two students holding my son and punching him in his stomach. My son was crying; other students were laughing. I was furious! Then, the students turned toward me and began to tease me. Again, the incident was never resolved. And once more I wondered: *What kind of culture is this where kids do not respect their elders? Who are these uncivilized people?*

Another day, there was a knock at our front door. When my husband answered, the men on our doorstep began laughing and making fun of my husband's turban and beard. He closed the door on them, but it was yet another humiliation. I thought: *Americans have so many hairstyles, why do they act this way toward our customs? And, in a civilized society, who dares to make fun of a person on the threshold of his home?*

Since we had resolved not to move back to India, I got on with my life. I went back to school and earned a certificate as a dental assistant, although I soon realized that I could not find a work shift that matched my kids' school schedules. The solution was for me to work within the schools. I pursued the idea of working in food service, but never found a job. Then, I learned about an opening as a Punjabi tutor with the Macomb Intermediate School District. This was a major milestone for me. I was proud that I could now pass a test in English to get that position!

Now, I could reach out to assist other newcomers—students as well as their parents. Having survived my own rocky transition into American life, I was now able to make other new families aware of helpful resources—some of which I wish I had known about when I arrived. As I shared my experiences with my colleagues in the school system, I also was able to help educators understand the key differences in our culture and traditions. That way, they could adapt their educational strategies to help all students—native-born Americans and newcomers—to accept the ever-increasing diversity in their classrooms. I began to participate in speaking engagements through the MISD, which highlighted cross-cultural and bilingual issues. I also agreed to help with workshops and other events designed to spread greater awareness of global diversity.

A friend finally introduced me to the women of WISDOM, where I felt that I was seeing the other side of the coin in American life. These women embraced differences and worked consciously to help newcomers feel welcome and accepted. As my own journey was unfolding, my sons and my husband developed their own approaches toward dealing with bias and bullying. Often, they simply ignored it. Most importantly, my sons excelled at school: They won competitions; they were invited into the National Honor Society and one son became a valedictorian. They were innovative and they inspired other students. As they gained the respect of others for their abilities, they also took time to help other students. Along the way, they made their own good friends. Eventually, they wound up at the University of Michigan, the University of Chicago, Harvard and MIT. From the very start, I had agreed to move to the U.S. mainly to provide them with educational opportunities. So, their success lifted my own sense of well-being in our adopted country.

Today, I am proud to be an American—a U.S. citizen. I love my country even though I recognize there still are challenges we must address. Today, immigrants still feel threatened in many corners of our country.

Over the years, I have doubled and redoubled my efforts to make our country the kind of place where all people can live together with dignity. With friendship and faith, I found a way to embrace my new home and to work toward making it the America of my dreams. Certainly, this has been a rocky journey, but we all share in this challenge. America can, indeed, be a heaven on earth—if we all work together.

CHAPTER 31

Raquel Garcia
Two Unlikely Sisters

She said, "Peace lives in the space between two people. That is where we practice our faith."

Raquel Garcia is the director of Partnerships and Community Outreach for Global Detroit, a major regional nonprofit. She cultivates support for immigrant integration and economic development initiatives such as homeownership, financial literacy, language access and access to higher education. Previously, Raquel was an immigrant-rights organizer and a campaign organizer. She spent 15 years in higher education in Detroit. She is passionate about leadership development among Latino youth and in LGBTQ communities. She also serves on the WISDOM board.

I HAD A job developing strategies to help immigrants and refugees integrate into the culture of the United States. Often, the challenges involve surface details like how to dress, how credit functions in the United States, or how to adapt their educational and professional records from their country of origin to properly translate their training and talents.

Many of the people I have met are hungry to learn. They are eager and excited to participate. Many of them seem to run with new vigor, as if they are freeing themselves from heavy weights that slowed them down in the past. They want to experience things like owning a home and opening a business—goals that may have been out of reach in their home countries.

As professionals tasked with helping them, we often defaulted to a mindset that we were "teaching them." About five years ago one of my students became the unlikeliest of teachers. Her first name is Amat and she is from Yemen. Her immigration documentation had expired. That is something we refer to as "out of status." This meant that her son was also out of status. She lived a very nervous life.

Even though I often worked with people experiencing immigration stresses and even though I empathized—I realized that I could never fully understand what it is like to live on the edge. In that situation, everything you know is transient and fleeting and could change at any minute. You can be picked up without warning, detained and deported. This can happen so swiftly that, often, families begin looking for missing relatives, not realizing they have been deported. It can take weeks to locate a person, get information, or even make contact with them.

As we continued to work together, I enjoyed Amat's company. Over time, I grew to love her as we laughed and worked in our sessions together. Then, one day I was concerned because I saw someone else taking a very different tone with Amat—talking down to her in an inappropriate way. The woman began talking very loudly, as if raising her voice would somehow bridge a communication gap between an English language learner and a fluent English speaker.

I felt rage in my heart. I advised Amat to snap back when someone addressed her like that in the future, and to build boundaries so she could limit the damage or hurt that others might inflict on her.

Amat had the most peaceful smile on her face and, as I went on, she repeatedly said, "It is OK. I am OK. It is OK." She went on to say that everyone was on their own path and that she was grateful for our work and our friendship. If she were to respond rudely to someone else, she felt she would be committing a kind of violence.

She told me that the peace of Islam is interpersonal. She said, "Peace lives in the space between two people. That is where we practice our faith."

In that moment, I examined my own faith and how I practiced it in my daily life. In that moment, her peace became my peace. I felt open to Islam and eager to learn more about how she practiced her faith in her daily life.

I have learned some words of Arabic so that every time I see Amat, I can greet her in her own language. Most recently, I learned the phrase, "*Alhamdulillah*," a common phrase in conversation with a Muslim friend. It means "praise God" in the way that Christians might use the phrase in talking about pleasant things that have happened recently. Another immigrant friend Karima taught me the phrase and giggled as I slowly learned how to properly pronounce it. I even recorded myself saying it over and over again so that I could practice. Karima was full of joy in teaching me. Usually, I was helping her to learn something. Now, the tables were turned and she was teaching her teacher. Then I realized: That's not quite what had happened in our surprising little transition. We actually had become each other's teacher—and each other's student.

I am also a student in my non-work life, re-learning Mexica, the indigenous Mexican practice of honoring the earth. In this time of way-finding, I also appreciate others' openness to the way I relate to and honor nature and my culture.

Because of Amat and Karima, I have become more curious and more willing to learn about Islam. I have also started thinking more about how I practice my beliefs in my daily life. Because of my friends, my work now includes taking what I am learning about Islam and speaking out when I encounter Islamophobia. From my work with undocumented families, I know that we all sometimes need the help of unlikely allies and friends. I am eager to help the vulnerable individuals and families I encounter now more than ever—thanks to the generous wisdom of my new unlikely sisters.

Part VI

Weaving
Creative Ideas

Want to make friends?
Become intentional about organizing opportunities.

CHAPTER 32

Edith Broida
Forming a Group of Explorers

If there is one thing that every group has in common, it's that it has experienced suffering. Maybe, if we learn more about how and why everyone has suffered, it would make all of us more compassionate.

Edith is a graduate of Wayne State University who began her teaching career in 1958 and retired from the profession 35 years later. Her religious beliefs vary, but she is a devoted member of both Temple Israel, which is a Reform Jewish temple, and the Birmingham Temple, which is part of Humanistic Judaism. An avid reader and current facilitator of book groups, Edith's choice of readings reflects her interest in different cultures and different faiths. Her interest in history led to the formation of The Museum Group, which offered more opportunities to learn about the beliefs of others.

MY EARLIEST MEMORY of an interfaith/intercultural experience was when I was in the eighth grade. I had a great friend, whose name was Connie, and she and I would talk about our differences; I was Jewish, and she was Greek Orthodox. This was after World War II, and everyone at that time was very conscious of being *American*. America was a melting pot, and Connie and I decided we would go to each other's church and synagogue.

I remember sitting there—the church was so new that there was still sawdust in the lobby—and suddenly, I smelled something. I leaned over to Connie and said, "Oh, no! I think the church is on fire!" She looked at her mother, and they smiled at each other: What I was smelling was incense! It just shows how we don't know much about each other's faiths, and how useful it would be to know more.

I went to a mostly Jewish high school until, in the tenth grade, my family moved to a blue-collar neighborhood. Suddenly I was different, and people would say things that they didn't know were demeaning to me. But my parents had moved a lot—seven times in my 12 years of school—so I was used to being different. At Wayne State University I joined a Jewish sorority, and later, I married a Jewish man.

Many years later, when an Arab-American Museum opened in Michigan, I came up with the idea of The Museum Group. I thought: We already have the Charles Wright African-American Museum and the Holocaust Museum in the Metro Detroit area. What would happen if I gathered a diverse group, and we would all go to one another's museums? With Deborah Smith-Pollard, an African-American woman, and Renee Ahee, a Lebanese-American woman, we formed The Museum Group. It wasn't Jews with Jews, Blacks with Blacks or Arabs with Arabs; we were all together.

In all three museums, we found an emphasis on American history—how the people came to America, and what they achieved. But if there is one thing that every group has in common, it's that it has experienced suffering. Maybe, if we learn more about how and why everyone has suffered, it would make all of us more compassionate.

At the Charles Wright Museum, we learned that when Africans were put onto the slave ships, they were given salt pork—a food staple that was so different from that in their regular diet that many of them died. The museum even had a simulation of a slave ship rocking, and we could hear moaning. It gave us a good idea of what it might have been like to be a slave.

After visiting the Charles Wright Museum, we went out to eat, which was our practice—this time at Ruby's Kitchen on Woodward, where we ate fried chicken, mashed potatoes and gravy. After all of our museum explorations, we ate ethnic food and allowed time to talk.

The Museum Group grew, and some, unknowingly, said things that ruffled feathers. Knowing this, I held a meeting at my house. I was disturbed that people were becoming uncomfortable with one another. As we talked and shared our feelings—becoming quite emotional—we said that if we can't get along, there's no hope for the rest of the world! We were now far more sensitive to how people felt, and the following year, we decided that it wasn't just our ethnic backgrounds that made us who we were, but also our religious backgrounds. We decided we should also visit one another's place of worship.

First, we went to a Lebanese-Christian church, and there, I was surprised that the services weren't that different from my own Jewish services. We then went to a church in Detroit, and it was great, with everyone dressed up and singing joyously. The pastor met with us after and arranged a brunch with hummus, bagels—food that he thought would be pleasing to all of us. We also went to an evening service at my temple. What I noticed was that the religious leaders in each of these places went out of their way to make us feel welcome.

I once read an article in *Real Simple*, an interview of women who were 100 years old or older. In this article, one woman said, "If there is a God, he is the God of everyone." And I thought: How true and logical this is. No one—whether Islamic or Catholic priest or Orthodox rabbi—can possibly own God. My temple has even taken out pronouns that refer to God as "Him." I liked this elderly woman's wise statement because it really spoke to a universal God.

Since most of the women in The Museum Group are professionals or traveling retirees, it's often hard for us to get together. Forming such a group is a challenge, but we have learned how valuable it is to visit historical museums and religious institutions together. We discover that we're not as different as we think!

In America, millions of immigrants did not know English when they arrived; they encountered prejudice; they faced enormous challenges; this is such a widespread story for so many families. Millions began here, in the U.S., as part of a first generation, learning the language and struggling through menial jobs—hoping to see that their children's lives would be better than their own.

I'd like to see our Museum Group become a model that is duplicated in school groups, PTAs, church groups, women's clubs and other organizations. Many of us have experienced great success in America. We need to learn our respective stories and broaden our world.

CHAPTER 33

Rehana Saleem Qureshi
Reaching Out and Reaching Within

If we had stayed inside our Muslim box, we would have grown anxious, afraid. Instead, we held Open Houses. We invited people to come inside.

Now 60 with a grown daughter of her own, Rehana reflects on a lifetime of navigating friendships both within the close bonds of the Muslim community and in the larger world of diverse cultures. Education is one key in forming such healthy relationships, she says.

WE MOVED FROM India to Pakistan when I was little. We had to make this difficult move with nothing—just the clothes on our backs. When we moved, we were four sisters, then three more sisters were born in Pakistan—so we were seven sisters in all. Through these years, we became a very close family.

Education is so important in life. My parents raised us in a home with Shakespeare and *National Geographic Magazine*. We read about new things in publications my father ordered from England. I remember my sisters and I would sit down together and read articles about how to do new things, like knitting, sewing and cooking new foods.

Eventually, my family decided to move to the U.S. and, over a period of about 10 years, relatives helped one another to migrate. I came in 1973. I got married and moved to Fort Wayne, Indiana. I studied to become a medical technologist and, for 22 years, I worked at the Detroit Medical Center in the microbiology department.

I am a moderate person. I'm very open to friends of different faiths and cultures. I worked in the medical community, so I have Christian, Jewish and Hindu friends and I know that we are all the same as people. We all have families and we all face problems in life—often in very much the same ways, whatever faith we may be.

As parents, my husband and I put a high value on education and carefully selected schools for our daughter. When our daughter was young, we chose a day care center called Kinderkirk, where she got along very well with children from other cultural and religious backgrounds.

As I was growing up, I attended Catholic schools through my college years. It was a good education and I found the nuns to be very dedicated. They helped to mold my character into the woman that I am today. But I was growing up in a Muslim community, in a Muslim country. My daughter was growing up in a country where most people are not Muslim. It is important to learn about your own faith.

So, my husband and I—together with many friends—began to work on establishing a Muslim center in Canton, a town west of Detroit, where we live. In the beginning, we would rent a hall when we got together or sometimes we met in someone's basement. Twenty-five or 30 families would gather for potlucks. We organized ourselves and worked on establishing our own place. The women helped to raise the money to build our school and community hall. This was difficult, but we knew that we were laying the foundation of our faith for our children, so we worked hard. One year we raised $80,000 by catering for all kinds of occasions like weddings and other events.

The families that helped were Muslim, but they also were diverse—from many different places. Some were Pakistani and Indian, some were Egyptian, others were Libyan. They were from many places.

My daughter studied for a number of years in a Muslim school, and she was a good student. Then, after eighth grade, we moved her to a Catholic school. She's quite athletic and, at her new school, she joined the track team and the ski team. Today, she continues those passions by running marathons and designing soccer shoes for a living. I am glad that she had this mix in her schooling. The Islamic schools helped her to hold onto values that come from our religion—like not drinking. With friends now, she often is the designated driver, because people know that she doesn't drink.

Some people have this idea that Islam is such a strict religion that its members can't even talk with people of other faiths; and that might be the case for some Muslims, but I am very broadminded, and I feel that people must interact with one another outside of their own little boxes.

If we don't do this, it is easy to become afraid.

When my Muslim community began building up the Muslim center in Canton, there was some community opposition around us from non-Muslims who wondered what this place was going to become. If we had stayed inside our Muslim box, we would have grown anxious, afraid. Instead, we held Open Houses. We invited people to come inside. We welcomed so many people that I remember going into a drug store one day and being surprised to find that a woman working behind the counter knew me already! The woman had come to one of our Open Houses and had enjoyed it so much that she greeted me in the store.

I know that not everyone is as open as I am, but I do think that this is the way to make the world a safer place for all of us. We need education. We need relationships with people from different countries and cultures. Once we make friends with people, they aren't just Muslims or Hindus or Christians—they become our friends.

Life is short. I'm 60 now. I look in the mirror and say: Oh, my! It's like I blinked my eyes and suddenly I am now this old. But even at my age, there is still work to do. God wants to strengthen us all in this way—through drawing us closer to one another. There is too much violence in the world today because of the ignorance between people. Every time I pick up a newspaper, I wonder: Where is all of this taking us?

In recent years, I joined this new group of educated women, WISDOM, so that I could learn more about other religious traditions. For example: Bahá'ís. I didn't know much about Bahá'ís before I joined WISDOM. And do you know what happened to me? This new group made me go deeper into my own religion! Now, I am always wanting to learn more so that I can talk intelligently to other people about Islam.

I know there are other women like me. Perhaps if more of us pursue learning and friendships that cross our many traditions, we actually *can* make a difference where we are living. And after that? Perhaps we can reach out beyond our own cubbyhole and make a difference across the country. And someday? We might be able to make a difference in the wider world.

CHAPTER 34

Sudha Chandra Sekhar
Dancing a Pathway to Heaven

When we arrived, everyone could see big differences between us: The Girl Scouts came in their simple uniforms, and my students in their elaborate dance costumes.

Sudha Chandra Sekhar was born in India and began her career at the age of 5 as an artist in *Bharata Natyam*, a form of dance with roots that go back thousands of years in Indian tradition. Her dance school, Hindu Temple Rhythms, was founded in 1958 by her parents. When Sudha married Sankarnarayan Chandra Sekha, an engineer, in 1967, the dance school moved with them to Canada, where she continued to perform and teach. The couple raised three daughters, who are

artists in their own right. In 1978, the Chandra Sekhars moved to Michigan, where "Sudha Aunty," as she is lovingly known, became a doyen of Indian classical dance and music in Michigan. A lifetime achievement honoree from Michigan Dance Council, Sudha embodies the Hindu spirit of pluralism.

THROUGHOUT MY LIFE, I have given more than 5,000 performances around the world and now I devote myself to teaching young aspiring dancers in southeast Michigan. I also teach theory classes for more advanced students, professionals and others interested in this ancient art from the Indian subcontinent. My artistic discipline in dance, *Bharata Natyam*, is deeply rooted in the *Natya Sastra*, ancient Vedic philosophies and Hindu spirituality.

When I began my studies in 1943 in India, we could all see that the alien British rule was in its dying days. India was at the threshold of independence. By the time I completed more than a decade of studies and training, India had attained its independence and my own early career paralleled the rise of our new nation's pride in our diverse cultures. In 1958, I was invited to perform at Rashtrapati Bhavan, New Delhi, for India's prime minister, Pandit Jawaharlal Nehru, as he was hosting New Zealand's prime minister, Walter Nash. I danced at the coronation of royalty, the Maharaja of the princely Indian state of Bhavnagar, and for a president, the late V.V. Giri, who became the fourth president of India.

When I got married and moved to Canada, I gave my first international charity performance at the University of Windsor in 1967, followed by national performance tours of the U.S. in 1968 and 1975. With my husband's support, I continued dancing in North America, and also began to teach—not only my three daughters Vidya, Anjali and Anandini—but a host of others. I expanded my teaching to Hindu temples and universities, conducting advanced dance camps and classes both in the U.S. and Canada. Given my own confidence in bridging cultures, I have always encouraged my students to follow a similar path. I want to help them also experience and transmit the oneness of humanity with confidence.

This is how I came to work with Nada Dalgamouni, the global education director of the International Institute of Metropolitan Detroit, established in 1919. According to its mission, the institute is "dedicated to working with foreign-born and with all Americans in the constant task of solving social problems, acculturation, education and acceptance. It provides and utilizes human and physical resources to advance the welfare and the integration of the foreign-born and their relatives; foster community awareness that varied cultures contribute to the richness of American life; and serve other organizations in the areas of its competence."

As I began to work with Nada, I found a kindred spirit. We brought together our respective backgrounds as immigrants and our commitment to sharing our cultures. Nada and her organization provided opportunities to emphasize the importance of Detroit's multicultural heritage. My students and I had a venue to showcase our art.

Over the decades, the memories that I have of the many programs that Nada and I coordinated at the International Institute include the following:

I took a group of my students during a summer dance camp to perform for a group of young Girl Scouts the same age. When we arrived, everyone could see big differences between us: The Girl Scouts came in their simple uniforms, and my students in their elaborate dance costumes. The Girl Scouts were primarily from predominantly white communities; my students were all of Indian origin. But most of my students were also Girl Scouts in their own communities, opting instead to do a summer camp to deepen their *Bharata Natyam*. After my students danced, the girls mingled with our hosts, shared snacks with them in the big hall at the institute, and realized they had more in common than the outward differences that they initially perceived.

Nada also organizes an event during Detroit's Noel Night, a traditional celebration held during early December that includes dance styles from around the world: Polish, French, the Far East, and more. Nada always pushes me to represent the Indian tradition, even though it is hard to get people to commit at that time of year. One year, I had students from the entire southeast Michigan region hurriedly come together to perform at the festivities. Not only were my own far-flung students meeting each other, but they also met dancers representing other global traditions. My dancers participated in the French dance, still wearing their own colorful Indian garb. They learned the history of early French settlements in Detroit. My young dancers and their mothers also connected with the Polish and Chinese dancers and their parents. In a multi-generational way, we were celebrating many of the diverse populations that had formed Detroit's unique cultural mix.

You also will find my students occasionally dancing on a Detroit river cruise, bringing their classical art form to the International Institute's summer program.

My students become my children, and I am always looking for ways to help them to navigate the frenzy of activities that Indian-American children are encouraged to pursue: academics, sports and various social clubs. Along with those essential pursuits, I encourage them to preserve and lift up our traditional arts, as well. Over time, I want them to recognize that our *Bharata Natyam* now is part of America's rich tapestry. This is very much in keeping with Hindu ideals of pluralism and the acceptance of diversity that I have valued throughout my life. As we describe our religious tradition: We believe in one God with many forms. We understand the whole world as one loving family: *Vasudaiva Kutumbakam*.

Even the strong friendship I have formed with Nada is a model to my students and their parents of what is possible if we embrace full participation in a vibrant, diverse American culture.

My passion for my dance has kept me close to God every moment. I am so grateful for that. I do believe that dance is what I would call my *bhajan* to God—my pathway to heaven.

CHAPTER 35

The Rev. Charlotte H. Sommers
Connections Through a Death in the Family

As we form friendships, we discover there are things we all share in life—like concern for parents.

The Rev. Charlotte H. Sommers is the pastor at Northminster Presbyterian Church in Troy, Michigan, and convener of the Troy Interfaith Group. In the larger community, she works to promote diversity, and her latest accomplishment was  working with the Troy Interfaith Group to create an Interfaith Labyrinth on the grounds of the Northminster Church. Labyrinths are not mazes intended to confuse the walker, but rather circular pathways that lead slowly but surely to a central point. Walking the labyrinth is a tool for prayer and meditation. The practice was developed centuries ago to blend prayer and movement, as in a pilgrimage. In her story, Charlotte talks about the vital relationships that form around such work.

IN THE TROY Interfaith Group, we commit ourselves to "invite people to gather, grow and give for the sake of promoting the common values of love, peace and justice among all religions locally and globally." We "believe that peace among peoples and nations requires peace among religions." —based on a statement by Hans Küng.

Our group hosts some major events during the year, and one of these is the National Day of Prayer, which we observe with an interfaith service. A few years ago in Troy, we had a controversy that made news headlines across the state. National Day of Prayer events often are supported by evangelical Christians, and here in Troy, a Hindu woman wanted to say a prayer in a public National Day of Prayer event, but was discouraged. This led a number of us to form the Troy Interfaith Group. I offered to host the Interfaith National Day of Prayer event at Northminster Church, where I am the pastor, which is how I got involved.

Now, there are several of us from the interfaith group who have lunch together every month. We just casually say it's time to get together for lunch and then we talk about all kinds of things, from books to politics to what's going on in our lives and our families. These friendships have developed as a result of working with the Troy Interfaith Group, which was a surprise to me; I didn't expect these deeper friendships to develop.

As we form friendships, we discover there are things we all share in life—like concern for parents. The first time I visited a Hindu friend's home for lunch, it was after she attended my mother's memorial service. I so appreciated her being there, and afterward, she invited me for lunch to talk about some things I had said in the service. As we shared that lunch, we talked about my parents, and we also talked about her parents. She told me that something I had said in the memorial service about my mother really impacted her. My mother had taught me that our feelings are not "right" or "wrong." Our feelings are real. We shouldn't try to correct or fix people's feelings. We shouldn't say, "Don't feel that way!" If we want to build good relationships, we should listen and not judge another person's feelings.

As our time together continued, this Hindu friend and I talked about all kinds of lessons we'd learned from our families. We talked about prayer. We talked about lots of things. It was wonderful.

There also were some Muslim women who called and said they wanted to come visit me after my mother died. They said this was part of their tradition; they visit with the person who is grieving. I was so moved by their thoughtfulness. It was a really wonderful thing to offer. Unfortunately, our schedules were such that we couldn't actually get together, but the fact that they wanted to come and visit with me was very meaningful. They weren't of the Christian tradition, but they were showing a sense of compassion—and they were showing me a traditional way that they expressed this compassion in their community. Their call and that idea inspired me.

These experiences have shown me that we need to spend more time together, talking with people of different traditions. We need to enlarge the circle of people who interact with one another. When the Troy Interfaith Group hosts an event like our National Day of Prayer service or our Interfaith Thanksgiving Day service, we are "preaching to the choir." Usually the people who attend are already on the bandwagon. It's the people who would never attend such an event that we are really trying to reach.

Closing off our lives—insulating ourselves from other faiths and cultures—is a dangerous choice. We can't escape the fact that we're a global community now. The more we learn about each other, the "healthier and wealthier" we all become.

CHAPTER 36

Paula Drewek
Journeys Toward Friendship

What I remember is that the experience started with sickness. … But, what an evening! What an evening!

Paula is Bahá'í and a retired professor of humanities and comparative religions. Now, she devotes much of her time to interfaith work and uses all that she has learned throughout her life to form new relationships and help others. Over the past two decades, she has made many trips to India to spend time at the Barli Development Institute for Rural Women in Indore.

WHEN YOU REACH a certain point in life, you realize that many individuals have made a difference in shaping the person you have become. Among those people in my life is a couple I met in 1993 when I first visited India: Janak and Jimmy McGilligan. Janak's a former Hindu who became a Bahá'í shortly before taking on a position at the Barli Development Institute for Rural Women. Jimmy is a Bahá'í from Ireland who was doing some community work in India when they met and, later, decided to marry. I met them on my first visit to India when I was doing research for my doctorate and I have since been back every three years because I can't bear to *not* be in touch with these wonderful people.

When I first arrived, Janak and Jimmy met me at the airport and it was a delightful meeting; we met, we hugged and they welcomed me. I was like a dear sister who had come to learn about them and the Barli Institute—and, of course, I do dearly love the Institute now because of the work it's done and the many lives it's changed.

Together, Jimmy and Janak help to run the place: Jimmy manages the farm and land, and Janak takes care of the program and curricula. In my visits, I usually spend anywhere from two weeks to a month. Although it may seem like a remote place from our American perspective, I've been amazed at how often I've met people from around the world who have been to their doors. Myself and people from India, China, Britain, Australia, America, Sweden—we all funnel through this Institute because, since it was founded in 1986, it has grown and become very well-known in development circles.

The women of the Institute continue to give me joy every time I go. They are rural—from village life, from low castes, generally between the ages of 15 and 25 and they don't even know the local language of Hindi. Our means of communication are very limited to things that are visual and auditory, because language isn't an option. We dance together, we sing together, and they take such joy in the ordinary things of life, like listening to a piece of music and picking tamarind from a tree. One time when I was there, we made tamarind pickles and rolled out papadums, and to these women, every little task was just so much fun. They do all of their cooking with solar cookers; they raise all of their food on the three acres that are cultivated as part of this Institute.

The one thing I remember the most is from my earliest visit. There were a couple of trips we took to places outside of Barli and, in one case, we went to a village that was very remote— about four hours away. The man in that village who had been a Bahá'í the longest had come right up to the door of the director's house to invite us to come and celebrate a holy day with his village. I had to ride in the back of a jeep for four hours over Indian roads and when I got there, I was carsick! But the people of this village were so welcoming.

We met outside, and they had a number of *charpoys*—traditional Indian beds made of woven strips in a wooden frame. They had brought these outside, arranged them around a fire and invited us to sit down. We did a lot of singing and we formed a procession around the village with big torches. After we had processed through the whole village, we came to an area where they had an oven in the ground, where they were cooking bread balls. I'm not sure that I could have eaten the bread balls or drunk the water, so I ate what we had brought along—a few things like peanut butter and jelly and graham crackers. But that whole celebration with the people of that village— everyone seated on the ground, with the fire going at night—was so filled with spirit and love and the joy of being together. I will just never forget it.

What sticks out in my memory is that the experience started with sickness—I felt really yucky after that awful ride along bumpy roads. But, what an evening! What an evening!

So, the people in that village—and friends like Jimmy and Janak—continue to teach me about the spiritual principles of unity and how to relate to people of different cultures. I continue to learn from friends like these.

CHAPTER 37

Patty and Elana Haron
Bringing Diversity Into the Schools

You can call me Suzie Sunshine for talking like this. I've gotten burned plenty of times because of my outlook on life, but I remain optimistic.

The Harons are a mother and daughter who are both involved in the WISDOM women's network, largely because of Elana's effort to start a diversity club at her suburban high school. The Haron family has long enjoyed friendships that cross religious and cultural boundaries, so upon entrance into high school, Elana already understood the value of diversity. But a dramatic experience in Israel with other teenagers prompted Elana to re-evaluate relationships at her high school back home. She was determined to help more people form cross-cultural friendships. Soon her mother, Patty, got involved in the project, too.

ELANA'S STORY:

I'VE GROWN UP within Judaism, but I didn't really appreciate this fully until I went to Israel in 2006. While I was there on a teen mission to the country, the Israel-Hezbollah war started and rockets came into northern Israel. We were visiting a *kibbutz* in that region when an explosion went off not far from us. We felt the vibration. I could hear people screaming, and first they had us gather in a cafeteria—then, they had us all get into a bomb shelter.

This was so scary that I thought: We are going to die.

But then I began to think: No, my ancestors are all around me, here in this land. I envisioned them around me like you might think of angels hovering around. Then, I knew we'd be safe. And we were.

I did have to leave the country early with my group because of the war, but this made a life-changing impression on me. Israel is the land of our heritage, and our hope of a peaceful trip to this homeland had ended in violence—in war.

At my school, when I got back home, I thought that we should start a diversity club. I wanted to bring people together and work toward peace in the world. I wanted more than handshakes. I wanted our relationships to mean something.

People are so segregated in the way they live their daily lives today: often, people are not even trying to meet or understand different people.

My idea for an organization at school started in a small way. At first, the vice principal didn't seem at all supportive of having a diversity club. As students, we said to one another: What do we do now? Our vice principal doesn't even want to help start something like this. Can we do it? We could see that this was going to be a long process. We had to figure out the next steps on our own.

So, the group began to meet. My brother—we're twins—was part of it and helped, too. We all got together at someone's house and we began to discuss what this group might do together. Even by participating in those meetings, we opened ourselves up to others. I'm Jewish, and some of my Jewish friends were part of this, but we stopped being just a group of Jewish friends. Now, we were talking together as Jews, Muslims, Christians and others, too. We brought in Brenda Rosenberg from WISDOM to help us. We started planning for speakers who would come into the school from different cultures and religious groups. We planned for a Muslim speaker and our first speaker in the schedule was a rabbi.

This wasn't easy. We faced problems. When the rabbi came to speak, one of the teachers started freaking out about things the rabbi was saying. Her emotional response then offended some of the Jewish students in the audience. Then, we were afraid to bring in our next speaker, the Muslim, because we feared the reactions we might get. We had hoped to proudly show off these speakers—really welcome them to our school, and have them share their wisdom with us. Instead, it was an uncomfortable experience—largely because of responses we got from the school staff.

The students were more open. My best friend is Catholic, for example, and she found the rabbi's talk very interesting.

We kept working at it. We kept meeting and we kept planning. We started out with maybe 10 or 12 people, and now I think there are 25 or 30 people. I moved on to college, but my younger sister is still in the school and now is the president of the diversity club.

Now that I've moved on to college, I realize that what we started was very important. I'm a sophomore now at the university and I realize that, at this age, we're already moving out into a much larger world. There are fewer people trying to arrange things in our lives, encouraging us to fit into particular groups. Now, it's our choice who we'll talk with, where we'll go and what friendships we'll form. Many people choose to stay within a little bubble of people who are just like them. But I've learned how important it is to reach out beyond that comfortable bubble. That's our hope for a better world.

PATTY'S STORY:

I've always tried to help out when parents were needed at school. Elana went to a Jewish school for some years, but then she went into a public school, so she—and I—had both kinds of experiences.

My family placed emphasis on the importance of simply trying to do the right thing each and every day. I grew up with a very strong commitment to being a fair person, an honest person—a person who would always stand up for what is right over what is wrong. I taught that to my own children.

The biggest question I've had about religion through the years is this: Religion is supposed to create harmony—so why does it often do the opposite? Originally, religion was supposed to unify people: to bring them together in communities and to establish rules that would guide people in fair and peaceful ways. But as religions developed over so many centuries, it seems as though religion now separates people more than it unites them. You can see the segregation in so many places. In a high school, just look at who sits together in the lunchroom: You'll see the separation right there.

So, when my daughter Elana wanted to start this diversity club—and her brother agreed to help her—I thought it was a good idea. There was a lot of thinking behind Elana's idea. She had been in Israel. She also had read *The Kite Runner,* and she saw in that book how people could be discriminated against even within their own religious group. She felt very strongly that she should start doing something about these problems.

I wanted to help my kids get the Diversity Club off the ground. But it's difficult for parents, too. You have to be careful and balance your own involvement.

This did take a whole lot of effort from the kids themselves. At first, many of the kids in the club were Jewish. They invited others to join the group, but it took time to grow and make new friends. Over time, it did open up and more kids got involved.

As a parent, I teach my children that the goal in life is to become a good person who helps other people. That's not the main message our culture sends to young people today. Have you watched TV shows like *Survivor*? There are so many messages on TV and in other media saying that life is all about competition—beat the other guy and win at all costs. As parents, we've got to show kids that there's an alternative to that kind of competition.

You can call me Suzie Sunshine for talking like this. I've gotten burned plenty of times because of my outlook on life, but I remain optimistic. I still believe it's important to encourage hope and cooperation among people. Sometimes, people aren't ready for that. But I keep working at it, because most people really are good—you just have to give them a chance to do the right thing.

I'm not naïve. I know what goes on, even among good kids—problems like cyber-bullying can become very painful. I've seen this firsthand, and I tell other parents that we have to be involved in our kids' lives.

So, as other parents read our story, I hope they will feel inspired to become active and to try ideas like a diversity club. Remember that it won't be easy.

But you know what? All you can do is wake up each morning and try to do the right thing.

ELANA'S FINAL WORD:

Now that I'm in college, I realize how important it has been for me to meet older women through groups like WISDOM. Women in WISDOM helped me even while I was in high school, working on our diversity club. Now, I realize how much I can learn from these women.

Just seeing them together, talking and working on things, is inspiring. When I see that—these women with so many differences in their lives working together—I realize that it is possible for adults to work together as friends. It is possible to stop focusing on things like the clothes each person wears or his or her religious background—and to focus instead on people's hearts. For me, it's a wonderful experience just to walk into a room and spend time with women like this.

CHAPTER 38

Brenda Naomi Rosenberg
The Courage to Follow a Vision Toward Peace

Sometimes tiny sparks trigger bombs;
sometimes they light candles.

Brenda is active in her Jewish congregation and in Jewish causes around the world. Her earlier career in fashion marketing gave her decades of experience in moving confidently across geographic and cultural boundaries. Here is her story of an idea—rooted in friendship—that is making a difference around the world.

I GREW UP around bright lights. My parents owned the Raven Gallery in Detroit, a meeting place for artists, musicians, writers and civic activists. In my 20s I began a long career in fashion marketing, and eventually was named vice president of fashion merchandising and marketing for Federated and Allied department stores. At the chain's height, I identified the trends that would show up in more than 1,000 stores—including Hudson's in Michigan, Bloomingdale's in New York, Burdines in Florida and Bullock's in California. I've traveled widely, rubbing shoulders with the rich and famous—I even dined in Monaco with Prince Rainier III—and to this day, I have friends from nearly every cultural background you can imagine.

But, my work over the last decade has taken more courage than anything I experienced in my business career. As a Jewish woman who cares about her Jewish community and about Israel, it was a controversial decision to devote my life after September 11, 2001, to bringing Christians, Muslims and Jews together.

It has not gotten any easier over the years! After the war between Israel and Hezbollah, keeping friendships on both sides of the divide took daring, stubborn determination and a clear vision that our hope for peace depends on maintaining all relationships. But that is where peace begins—in the relationships we form as we break bread together, share our stories with each other and begin to work together. That's when the light begins to shine.

We have to look closely for those first flashes of light. Sometimes tiny sparks trigger bombs; sometimes they light candles.

One of those sparks flashed in my life after a lunch with my friend Imam Abdullah El-Amin, who is assistant imam at Detroit's largest Muslim center. We are unlikely friends: He's a 6-foot-6-inch male African-American Muslim leader and I'm a 5-foot-3-inch female Jewish peace activist; he's based in the heart of Detroit and I'm based in the suburbs. After an interfaith luncheon in the spring of 2003, we walked to our cars and continued to talk about all of the problems in the world that involve Jews, Christians and Muslims. "If we would only remember that we all share the same father, Abraham," Abdullah said to me, "then we might find ways to bring our family back together again." He reminded me of a passage in the Bible in which Abraham's two sons—Ishmael and Isaac—had been separated for many years. In spite of that, they came together at Abraham's death to bury their father. Then, Abdullah said to me: "We're tearing our world apart today. Why can't we do what Ishmael and Isaac did, and come back together as a family?"

All that day, I thought about his words. I couldn't stop thinking about Ishmael and Isaac reuniting, after all the hurt and anger they felt toward each other.

That night, I had a dream about a stage in a theater. On it, I saw Isaac and Ishmael leaving the caves of Machpelah—the burial site of Abraham—together. As they started to turn away from each other, the Archangel Raphaella flew in from stage left and wrapped her wings around the grieving brothers, asking them to sit down. She guided them through a four-step healing process.

The following week I met with Abdullah and another friend, the Rev. Dan Buttry, who is head of global reconciliation for American Baptist Churches. We felt that my dream could evolve into a new kind of peace initiative that would give us the opportunity to bring our fragmented communities together. We could tell the story of Abraham and his two sons, Isaac and Ishmael, in a new light. We could take the 2,000-year-old sibling rivalry, the brothers' posturing for a father's love, the demands for a fair share of the inheritance—both in terms of land and ideology—and retell the story to help people heal the trans-generational wounds that have imprisoned us in a cycle of fear, hate and intolerance. The idea for *Reuniting the Children of Abraham* was born.

Our next step was to find Metro Detroit teenagers from all three faiths willing to share personal stories about their experiences with the boundaries of faith and ethnicity. We were shocked to hear that every teen had been subjected to some form of religious, cultural or racial prejudice. Many already had developed a real fear of the "other." We used the four-step process of reconciliation with these teens: Step 1, breaking bread together, which turned into sharing pizza; step 2, sharing our deeply personal stories with the group, including ways in which we have been hurt; step 3, having someone else retell our stories; and step 4, collaborating on a project, which became *Reuniting the Children of Abraham*. From the beginning, it was far more than a theatrical production. We extended the experience into sessions during which the audience could talk with the young actors and with one another about the ideas we were presenting. We saw we had the potential to help communities not only in Michigan, but across the country and around the world.

That expansion took a whole lot of friends! Victor Begg, co-chair of the Council of Islamic Organizations of Michigan, encouraged two of his children, Sofia Begg Latif and Yousuf Begg, to take part in the original workshop. My friend Julie Cummings was supportive from the beginning, and her family and my family were among five—Cummings, Seligman, Farbman, Gershenson and Rosenberg—that donated funds to produce *Reuniting the Children of Abraham*. Entire cities got involved. The Kalamazoo-based Fetzer Institute both funded and brought a production to Kalamazoo and worked hard to bring many different groups together in its region of Southwest Michigan.

Media professionals joined our ever-widening circle. The CBS television network produced a documentary about the project that aired nationwide, and we were featured in an hour-long special on Bridges TV, a national Muslim television network.

Reuniting the Children of Abraham now has friends all around the world. In 2006, we were asked to speak to more than 400 psychologists and psychotherapists from 70 countries at the New Ways of Looking at Conflict Conference in Israel. While there, we also met with Arab and Israeli high school students who participate in a similar project called "Peace Child Israel." They were shocked to learn that the Middle East conflict affects high school students in the U.S.

The project has opened many doors. Imam Elahi gave me the honor of being the first Jewish woman to deliver a Ramadan sermon at a mosque in Michigan. Imam Abdullah El-Amin and I were keynote speakers at the 2006 National Humanities Conference in Louisville, Kentucky. In Atlanta, we spoke to more than

300 Jewish educators, most of whom had never met an imam. In 2007, I orchestrated an invitation for Victor Begg to address a national conference of rabbis—and Victor arranged for me to present *Reuniting the Children of Abraham* at the Islamic Society of North America, a gathering of more than 50,000 Muslims. In 2008, we were guests of the royal family in Amman, Jordan, where we presented the documentary in Arabic. That Arabic translation was a gift of another friend, Mona Farouk, whose story also appears in this book.

The project since 2005 has been packaged as a multi-media tool kit for peace, complete with a CD of educational material and a 40-minute documentary on DVD. That's all part of the ongoing website: http://www.brendanaomirosenberg.com/children-of-abraham.htm. Through all of this work and all of these travels, what interests me most is the question that started me on this long journey: Where can we find those individual sparks of light? I'm always looking for the change we can make in each life and each new friendship.

In 2004, our project became part of the first Midwest Palestinian-Jewish Dialogue Weekend (organized by more good friends, Len and Libby Traubman), held in Duluth, Minnesota.

At this dialogue weekend, we gathered in a circle to tell our stories. There was a young Muslim Palestinian woman who had arrived for the weekend with a very skeptical view of what we might achieve together. She retold her story of growing up in a refugee camp. She spoke of hardships and she shared how terrified she was of Israeli soldiers. She had witnessed a soldier shooting a child in the arms of a mother. At one point, she burst into tears and said she hated Jews.

She left the group and nearly left the entire program. I encouraged her to remain—and she did. As we had listened to her stories in our circle, she now took the time to hear Jewish stories. She learned about the Holocaust for the first time from a survivor. We shared a great deal more in the next two days, but most importantly, we shared our desire to work toward peace. This young woman sat next to me as we watched a presentation of *Reuniting the Children of Abraham*. We cried together for the past, but we also shed tears of hope for what the future might hold. After the presentation she asked for the microphone and said: "When I arrived on Friday, I hated Jews. I thought this weekend was going to be a waste of time. But now I know Palestinians and Jews can talk. I know now that peace is possible, and I can even call a Jew my friend"—and she gave me a hug in front of 600 people.

That's what renews my courage. That's the kind of miraculous spark I keep searching for wherever I travel around the world. That's the pathway of friendship that leads to peace.

CHAPTER 39

Gail Katz
A Journey Outward— and Inward

> *How can I describe the pleasure that I get watching the faces of 150 seventh-graders, their parents and their teachers, as we come together with rabbis, imams, priests and other clergy?*

Gail is an educator whose talents have led her to help found—or to dramatically reshape—various community groups, programs and activities over the years. In her story, she explores the roots of that creative activism. She also explains how this daring embrace of diversity has deepened the core of her own faith.

AS AN INTERFAITH activist, I'm often asked where my ideas and my energy for this work originated. To trace my long journey toward the creative ideas that now define my life, I have to travel back to my years growing up in a post-war, secular, Jewish family. You may not be Jewish yourself, but you may find yourself connecting with such early memories. Throughout my life, I've met many adults whose attitudes toward diversity were shaped when they were very young. I spent my early childhood and my elementary school years in Silver Spring, Maryland, in a rather non-Jewish neighborhood. I was one of a few Jewish children in my school. The memories that have stuck with me are ones of feeling different from my neighbors and my classmates. I started each morning bowing my head with all the other children and saying the Lord's Prayer in my public school classroom, and even in my sleep today I can recite "Our Father, who art in Heaven, hallowed be thy name ..." But I knew, deep inside me, that this was really not my prayer. At Christmastime, we had Christmas plays and sang songs like *Silent Night, Oh Come All Ye Faithful* and *Joy to the World*. Although I sang along, I knew that these were not my songs.

Every year I had to bring in my family menorah and explain the meaning of Hanukkah. For an extremely shy child, this was absolute torture—singled out in front of the class as different. I begged my mother to buy us Glass Wax, made by Gold Seal, so that my brother and I could participate in the same traditions as my classmates and make snowflake stencils on the windows, since we were not allowed to put up a Christmas tree.

My Judaism mostly revolved around holidays. We would go to the synagogue on Rosh Hashanah and Yom Kippur, and we had the family over for Passover and Hanukkah. I had no idea about other Jewish holidays, and when I was taken to our synagogue in Montgomery County, Maryland, my memories were again about feeling different and uncomfortable. My family only sent my brother to Hebrew School to prepare for his bar mitzvah. Girls were not expected, in the 1950s, to get any real Jewish education. So, as a child, I felt conspicuous for not knowing how to read or recite the Hebrew prayers. I would sit next to my father, playing with the *tsitsit* (the fringes) on his *tallit* (prayer shawl), waiting impatiently to go home. There was always this sense of anger inside me that I didn't fit in at school or in my Jewish community.

When I was 12 years old, my father got a job with Ford Motor Company and we moved to Oak Park, a suburb of Detroit. In 1960, Oak Park had a sizable Jewish population, and my junior high school was about 85 percent Jewish. My junior high school years were difficult ones for me: I still felt different, even though I was now in classes with many Jewish students. I was a target for bullying as the "new kid," the "quiet kid" and the "all-A" student. My sense of outrage at not being given respect for being different from the "cool" kids laid the foundation for my later passion in helping students organize diversity clubs.

While all of this was unfolding, my mother's father came from Far Rockaway, NY, to live with us. My Grandpa Aron was very religious, spoke mostly Yiddish, and reminisced with my mother about the old country. His world was the old Russia, which was taken over by Poland by the time my mother was born, and is today part of Belarus. I loved him dearly. Although we had a hard time communicating with words, we did just fine with kisses and embraces, and I have to admit that I picked up quite a bit of Yiddish along the way.

I learned from my grandfather about his world of Eastern European Jewry, his love for the Torah, his need to keep kosher, his *davening* (praying) and his Jewish custom of putting on *tefillin* (phylacteries) every morning in his bedroom. Our Passover Seders became very traditional, and to this day we sing out my grandfather's Eastern European Jewish prayers from the Haggadah (Passover prayer book) every year. I grew up with Holocaust stories—my mother's cousins, aunts and uncles had perished in the concentration camps—and I knew that my mother was alive only because my grandfather had the foresight to get his family out of Poland in the late 1920s.

My mother and father made their children keenly aware of our calling as Jews to *Tikkun Olam* (repairing the world). There were Russian Jewish immigrants at our Passover Seders every year. My mother and I marched together in Washington, DC to highlight the urgency of bringing persecuted Jews from the former USSR to the United States. During my senior year in high school, my family housed a foreign exchange student from Brazil and we talked often about championing the rights of African Americans in the South.

Because of my grandfather's and my mother's immigrant family background, I was drawn toward a career of teaching English to immigrants. From the time I graduated college, I spent my time teaching English as a Second Language to adults, and then finally teaching children in public schools. I saw how these students felt ostracized because of their struggle with the English language, their different cultures and religions, and their different economic status.

I formed a diversity club called STARS (Students Taking a Right Stand) to help address these problems, among others. We addressed all of our differences, celebrated our diversity, and learned how to stand up and speak out against bullying. We ran Family Heritage Fairs, displayed portraits of Holocaust survivors, sponsored No Name Calling Week and Mix-It-Up at Lunch Day, and put together an Ellis Island simulation for the entire school, to highlight everyone's cultural heritage.

It was during my teaching career in the Berkley School District that I noticed an article in the Jewish News about a grant that the Jewish Community Relations Council received to sponsor a Religious Diversity Initiative. It didn't take long for me to get on the committee, then chair the committee, and finally become the coordinator of the program entitled the Religious Diversity Journeys for Seventh Graders, which is now run by the Michigan Roundtable for Diversity and Inclusion. This wonderful program for seventh-graders in six school districts in Oakland County, just north of Detroit, promotes greater awareness and understanding of the many religions prevalent in metro Detroit and prepares students for life in our increasingly diverse society.

In the program, 25 students from each of the six school districts participate in five school-day field trips between January and May to focus on the differences and similarities among some of the major religions found in our community, including Christianity, Judaism, Islam, Hinduism, Buddhism and Sikhism. We visit a different array of temples and other houses of worship each year.

How can I describe the pleasure that I get watching the faces of 150 seventh-graders, their parents and their teachers as we come together with rabbis, imams, priests and other clergy to expand our horizons as a community?

A big step along my own journey was the nationally-known World Views Seminar at the University of Michigan-Dearborn. Each year, men and women from across the country enroll in this intensive, short-term program that immerses people in a wide range of religious traditions, including visits to many houses of worship. This academic program further fueled my passion to promote diversity, and I was drawn toward another widely-known program: the annual World Sabbath for Religious Reconciliation, held each January at Christ Church Cranbrook, a historic landmark here in Michigan. I got so involved that I wound up as chairperson of the planning committee.

Before I got involved, the Sabbath focused on prayers for world peace by the clergy of different religious institutions, but we shifted our focus toward youth—letting them actually lead the rest of us in prayers for peace, entertaining us with dance and music and creating peace banners that are woven into a Children of Peace Quilt.

In March of 2006, I met my spiritual soul mates: Trish, a Christian, and Shahina, a Muslim, at Brenda Rosenberg's *Reuniting the Children of Abraham*, a unique theatrical experience about connections between Judaism, Christianity and Islam. With my soul mates, I became one of the co-founders of WISDOM— Women's Interfaith Solutions for Dialogue and Outreach in MetroDetroit—a story you'll read elsewhere in this book.

What's most remarkable about my journey is that it has not led me away from my own faith! On the contrary, my quest has strengthened and deepened my Judaism.

In championing and celebrating "the Other," I have reconnected with my own childhood yearning. I have come full circle—from the days of feeling "left out" as a youngster, to conquering that feeling by enrolling as an adult in a Torah study class and attending Jewish retreats. I am awed by this turn in my long quest—taking me home even as it has carried me so far from my home.

My journey continues—outward and inward. Wherever you live as you are reading this, think about starting a journey of your own. You're likely to find your own tradition enriched even as you reach out to explore the larger world with others.

CHAPTER 40

Raman Singh
Learning We Are One, After All

They start out seeing only differences.
Soon, they discover the similarities.

Raman Singh is a leader in education and interfaith relations in southeast Michigan as well as a participant in her own Sikh community. She is a past trustee of the West Bloomfield School District and, in 2017, is president of the Interfaith Leadership Council of Metropolitan Detroit (IFLC), where she focuses much of her time on the IFLC's education and grant-advisory committees. She also has two grown sons, one of whom was key to Raman's story.

I FIRST HEARD about interfaith relations from my father, who participated in such gatherings when I was in high school and college. When I heard him describe these diverse meetings, breakfasts and prayer services, the idea made sense to me. As Sikhs, we need to counter bias by letting other people know more about our faith and culture. When I began to participate myself, I discovered that this was not just a matter of representing our own tradition in such settings. There was a lot we could receive as a result of our involvement.

As American Thanksgiving approaches, religious leaders across metropolitan Detroit usually organize a large interfaith service. When I began to attend that annual event, I was inspired to hear all of the different prayers! Along with the other sacred voices from cultures that circled the globe, I would hear our own Sikh *Ardas*, supplicatory prayers for God's help that we offer at almost every Sikh gathering. Our voices were welcomed as part of the community's sacred chorus of prayer.

Over time, the number of interfaith organizations and initiatives increased in our region and the number of events and opportunities multiplied. Occasionally, I agreed to represent our community in programs at churches, schools and with senior citizen groups. I was pleased to be contributing, step by step, to a wider appreciation of our heritage as Sikhs.

When my son Simren was in the seventh grade, he was selected through his school to participate in a new educational program called Religious Diversity Journeys. Learning about world religions is a mandated subject in the public school social studies curriculum at that grade level. No one was required or pushed to participate in this supplemental program. It was optional and kids had to be recommended by their teachers, then they had to receive their parents' approval. Today, the program has grown into a nationally respected model for learning about global religious cultures in a neutral, balanced and accurate way. However, at the time Simren was invited to participate, I had never heard of the program and decided to talk with his counselor.

"What world religions are included?" I asked. When I was given the list, I noticed our own faith was not a part of this overview of religions.

"I like what I am seeing here, but you should include Sikhism," I told the counselor. "If you need some help, let me know."

That casual offer to help led to a telephone call from Gail Katz, who helped to develop Religious Diversity Journeys—and also was a co-founder of WISDOM. After introducing herself, Gail said, "I've heard you're willing to help. Would you present a talk about Sikhs?"

How could I refuse? My first invitation was in a middle school gymnasium where the students enrolled in that year's class had gathered. I remember focusing on cultural aspects of our traditions: music, dance and visible articles of our faith, like the turbans Sikh men wear. There were lots of questions, including: "So, how long does a man's hair get?" And: "What happens if you want to marry someone who is not a Sikh?"

Over the years, I got much more involved in the program and in developing the overall curriculum. In fact, I'm now involved in running the program. I am currently serving as president of the Interfaith Leadership Council of Metropolitan Detroit (IFLC), the regional nonprofit that leads Religious Diversity Journeys. We work with 700 seventh graders from 25 schools. That grade level is a wonderful time to explore this aspect of social studies, because the girls and boys are old enough to understand the concepts, but any biases toward other cultures are not yet set in stone. The kids are eager to learn and are remarkably open-minded. These students in the program act like ambassadors, carrying what they have learned back to schools across southeast Michigan.

Parents play important roles and often form their own cross-cultural friendships as a result. Here's how that process unfolds: First, parents learn about the program before a child can even enroll. The adults have to give their approval. Then, we invite parents to volunteer as chaperones and drivers on a half dozen field trips we take each year. The parents love to join in and sometimes we have other family members and caregivers take part, as well. Because of the strong parental interest in the seventh-grade program, the IFLC more recently has added a very popular series of programs for adults called Exploring Religious Landscapes. One series looked at four different religions; another focused on the various branches of Judaism; and yet another explored denominations within Christianity.

These programs are full of what I call "aha" moments. You can see the awareness spread through a diverse crowd of children or adults when they learn the reasons that Sikh men wear turbans or Jews chant a particular prayer or Christians follow an ancient ritual. They start out seeing only differences. Soon, they discover the similarities. In their excitement, the worry of encountering strange new people and places evaporates. They lower their guard and want to learn more about others around them. As they relax, they make new friends.

The biggest impact we have on these kids' lives is to open their eyes to the fact that the world around them is not monolithic—one of the most basic goals in a standard social studies curriculum. We are experienced educators and take great care with every aspect of the program. We carefully select all presenters and train all of the adult participants. We make sure that each part of the program focuses on appropriate educational material. We don't do any proselytizing. No one is encouraged to join a new faith. Educators in the public schools continually look over our curriculum and approve the material. There are lots of checks, balances and safeguards built into the program.

What this provides for the students and the adult participants is a remarkable opportunity to discover the shared values that connect people in religious and cultural communities across America. We all may look and sound quite different to each other, but many core American values unite us.

This began as a personal mission for me—a way to help combat the bullying of Sikh young people. As a mother of Sikh sons, I had a personal stake in helping more Americans understand enough about our culture, so that meeting a Sikh is not an awkward encounter.

Now, I think of my work in a larger context. First, as helping Sikh kids everywhere avoid bullying, but, as the years have passed, I know that I have received as much as I have given through these new connections across the larger community. This process has led to many new friendships for me, as well as for my children. Initially I met Gail Katz, then many of the educators and parents in participating schools, and eventually I met my colleagues in the IFLC. Every year, new friendships form.

On an even more profound level, these relationships have deepened my own faith, and I like to think that along the way, I have helped to deepen the faith of people I have met. This is especially true as I encounter more and more people who join in this interfaith work with unselfish motives. I realize that they are joining in our collective efforts, not to gain something, but because this kind of work is a natural expression of their core values. Now, I think of my own vulnerabilities in a new way. I began my involvement, years ago, out of a selfish sense of wanting my family to fit in more easily. But, I have learned that people of all faiths have vulnerabilities, including a yearning simply to be respected and included in the larger community. When we work together, we can call upon a stronger collective power to address these concerns. I consider myself fortunate to have gained this perspective and, ultimately, I realize that this connects with the highest values in my own religious tradition. Sikhs are called to see the One in everyone.

What better way to gain that enlightenment than to learn about the "other"—and to realize that "they" are *you*, after all.

Part VII

Widening Our Vision
of the World

Through the eyes of friendship, we glimpse a hopeful new world.

CHAPTER 41

Elaine M. Schonberger
Handing Down an Awareness of Community

It opened their eyes, just as we had hoped.

Elaine is an educator and a community activist who often volunteers her time to promote diversity and human rights. She is able to look across nearly a century of her own Jewish family's life in the U.S.—and see a legacy of cross-cultural relationships.

INTERFAITH RELATIONSHIPS HAVE been around for a long time in America; they have been a part of my family since before I was born, in the 1950s. They are the means by which my parents related to their community, whatever the religion or race or ethnicity of our neighbors was. As children, we were taught to be extremely respectful of other people and to help anyone who needed our help—this was the lesson in our home from Day 1.

My father, Izzy Malin, devoted his life to these relationships. He was a businessman—a salesman in the wholesale food business—and he understood that everyone should pitch in to help the community. As we were growing up in northwest Detroit, I remember my parents volunteering in community efforts at local Catholic parishes as well as in the Jewish community. Over the years, my parents were honored by Catholic leaders for their efforts. My father had Arab-American friends, some of whom were Christian and others Muslim. He met them through the grocery business, and he was known for helping these friends get their grocery stores started, in many cases.

In 1982, my father and my mother, Frances, helped to found the American Arab and Jewish Friends. Today, we're seeing new approaches to diversity in groups like WISDOM, but the Friends group my parents co-founded was very important for many years. Their group brought together a lot of business people and community leaders to do good things together.

My husband and I lived in Texas in the 1980s, but when we moved back to Michigan in 1990, I saw more of the work they were doing firsthand. I got involved in similar efforts myself, working on projects like United We Walk, which was an annual Martin Luther King Day observance. I was also the only parent on a multicultural committee in local schools; the other members of the committee were educators and staff members.

One good idea my parents helped to get started through the Friends group was an essay contest for high-school students. The contest was quite involved: Each year, the Friends group sent out packets to local schools, inviting students to apply for this scholarship competition. Then, the Friends group would help interested students organize themselves into groups of three—usually including a Christian, a Muslim and a Jew. The three would have to complete a number of activities together over several months: They had to visit each of the three homes, and experience a meal of foods that were typically a part of each cultural group; they would visit one other's place of worship, too. Then they would prepare their final essays. Each student had to write an essay about his or her personal experience—and then they would write a fourth essay, "The Ties That Bind," with input from all three students. We usually got 25 or 30 of these completed packets each year.

I always knew that the scholarship competition was an important program and, after my father died in 1999, I volunteered to help lead the Friends group and coordinate the essay contest for a while. The group no longer exists, but in the year 2000, I had a chance to see what a big impact the essay contest had on my own family.

My son, Michael, was a senior, and he wanted to complete the "Ties That Bind" project. He found two other students to join him: One was a Muslim and one was an Iraqi-American Christian.

I still remember the night they came to our home. My mother visited just to be a part of it that night. This was a program she and my father had started years before, and her grandson, Michael, was going through it now with other students. I fixed chicken soup with matzo balls, a brisket and some other traditional dishes. I served them gefilte fish. My mother and I were thrilled to see this.

In the final essays, each student talked about what he learned, but what impressed me was the way they all found similarities between our cultures. Even in our places of worship, they realized that many of the prayers and blessings were similar. It opened their eyes just as we had hoped.

I was born into interfaith work. This was just a part of life in my family. My parents always understood that a healthy community depends on various faiths, races and cultures all working together. They saw this, partly because they were in business and they understood the networks that can make this country a better place for everyone. And I thank God now that they had those insights. They didn't teach me tolerance—that was not enough. They taught their children acceptance and appreciation and the importance of joining hands to work together.

Unfortunately, the world has changed in many ways. The Friends group doesn't exist anymore. The scholarship program ended, although I think the idea is still a good one. These days, fewer people have the time—or take the time—to work on this kind of outreach that we once saw as so vital.

But I certainly hope that the larger legacy I inherited—passed along to my sons Michael and Keith—is not over. I know my sons now are involved in groups that promote these same goals. My husband, Mark, and I are very proud of them. My parents would be as well. We need to keep forming strong relationships like this in each new generation. The work needs to continue.

CHAPTER 42

Katherine Nyberg
Enlarging Our Spiritual Vision

Initially, my exposure to this ancient spiritual tradition felt odd. Is Buddhism even a religion?

Katherine is a lifelong educator and past chairperson of the Ecumenical Theological Seminary in Detroit. She is active in interfaith groups, including WISDOM, and is drawn especially to the deeper theological connections shared by men and women of different faiths.

A LIFELONG PRESBYTERIAN, I follow the denominational identity of my Scottish foremothers and forefathers. We attended Church regularly where my mother taught Sunday school. But, I was never taught that my denomination had a corner on truth, and for that I am grateful.

I grew up in Detroit with Catholic and Protestant neighbors, and while there weren't many Jewish people on our block, one of my mother's closest friends was the wife of a Jewish high school math teacher who lived a few doors away from us. That couple served as foster parents to several girls, and I was frequently in their home meeting a newcomer so that I could then introduce her to the kids on the block.

When I was a public high school teacher, many of my colleagues and my principal were Jewish and we taught a diverse population of children from homes representing more than 80 languages. Our students' families came from lands including Lebanon, Iraq, Albania, Japan, Mexico and Israel. In our classrooms, these nations and cultures became much more than mere dots on a world map.

As a middle-aged adult, I met several Muslim women and men, shared meals and stories, and felt connections to their faith through our shared Abrahamic roots. Toward the end of my 30-year teaching career, I began lecturing in a public university with many Muslim students. My world broadened even more as they so generously, often with great humor and always with tenderness and respect, shared their stories.

So, my Abrahamic "circle" felt complete and comfortable.

Then, a special person in my life introduced me to Buddhism, tugging at the perimeter of my Abrahamic circle. Initially, my exposure to this ancient spiritual tradition felt odd. Is Buddhism even a *religion*? Does it have a theology? Is there room for God in Buddhist practice? Is "love thy neighbor" as fundamental to Buddhist practice as it is to the Abrahamic faiths? Or, is Buddhist practice one of interior discipline and discernment?

My questions were answered in a jolt of understanding. The Buddhist term "nondual" is used to describe the very nature of creation. Nondual thinking is rich and deep in Buddhist thought, and I am not equipped to address this vast subject here, but it did initially challenge my "me here, God there" image of reality.

At the same time, voices in my Christian faith were positing a similar nondual vision, based on a reemergence of early church doctrine. For clarity, let me offer some observations of Catholic Franciscan friar Richard Rohr: "Previous philosophers said God was *a* Being, which is what most people still think today." Instead, "God is being itself ... waters, plants, animals, humans, angels, and God. We all participate in the same being. ... This gives us a foundation for understanding the sacredness of everything and our connection with everything. We are already connected."

Then came my moment of understanding. It happened late one afternoon in the hot Mexican sun. Children were cooling off in the pool—splashing, doing handstands, and floating on plastic dinosaurs. Slowly a raccoon approached the pool. It lurched sideways seeking water. A mother noticed, screamed, and the children were hustled into the protection of the house.

A couple of the adults tried to shoo the raccoon away, but it seemed unfazed until one man took a broom and made sweeping gestures at it. It backed away and staggered down the beach to rocks at the water's edge. There, exhausted, it seemed to take refuge.

The children thought the raccoon was merely resting. We adults knew better. This poor animal was in great distress.

As the sun set, dinner was ready. People gathered in the dining room. The room quieted as a child recited words of gratitude. Her recital ended with "amens" and "indeeds" from around the table. A platter of chicken was served, followed by plates of grilled vegetables and bowls of fruit. The room filled with the clatter of knives and forks, conversations, and laughter. Several moments later, I noticed the lone Buddhist in the room slip out with a piece of chicken in a napkin. He returned a few minutes later without the chicken.

My questions about Buddhism were answered. My Abrahamic circle split open.

CHAPTER 43

Ellen Ehrlich
Freeing Friends from Boxes

*In accepting all people, our community
becomes a reflection of the real world.*

Like millions of Americans, Ellen has moved through a wide range of religious experiences in her life. Born into a New York Jewish family, she moved through Christian Fundamentalism, home churches and even a period of secular inactivity. Today, she's active in a diverse Episcopal Church in Royal Oak, a city north of Detroit. Similarly, Ellen's professional career has ranged widely from years as an American media executive in print publications and network TV news—to her current work as a Realtor. Her breadth of experience has led her to deeply appreciate the rare value of nonjudgmental acceptance in friendship.

"WHAT ARE YOU?"

When someone asks me that question about my religious affiliation, I remember something a friend told me back while I was involved in a house church in New York. That day I was very upset about something that had happened, and my friend Bob told me: "Never let anybody put you into a box."

I have tried to live my life that way—by not putting myself into a box and not putting anyone else into a box. The problem is that as soon as we're stuck in a mental box, or we put other people in a box—whether it's a professional, theological, spiritual, sexual or political box—then that's how you're defined in another person's mind. And you're never going to get back out of that box, in most cases. You're stuck.

If you do that to other people, then it's hard to be fully accepting.

I was born Jewish. Now, I say I'm an Episcopalian. I don't say I'm "Christian"—that word describes a particular box for most people. Sometimes I do have fun with these ways of defining myself. In church, I remember someone saying that, spiritually speaking, "We're all 'adopted.'"

I said, "No, you might be 'adopted.' I was chosen!"

It's important to be aware of these boxes, because there are a lot of people eager to push others into them for their own purposes. Back in the 1980s, when I was working for NBC News, I went back and forth to Los Angeles each year. Once, a friend invited me to visit a church on Wilshire Boulevard in Beverly Hills. It turned out to be this nondenominational church with a rock band on stage and, soon, people around me were speaking in tongues. At that point I was sliding down in my chair, trying to be invisible, because I didn't want to be around these people. But the whole thing works on you. At the end, the minister on stage asked, "Does anybody here want to accept Jesus Christ as their Lord and Savior?" And, my hand went up! I always want to deny that I actually raised my hand, but it happened. My hand went up! The next thing I knew, I was taken someplace where people were praying and talking to us about starting Bible studies and I was already saying to myself: It's going to be OK. I'm going back to New York soon. It's going to be OK.

My church now, St. John's Episcopal, is the perfect church for me. Here, everyone is accepted. Everyone is welcome. We have a sign that says "You are welcome" and at this church, we mean it. There are people who drive long distances to attend this church.

In accepting all people, our community becomes a reflection of the real world. We have people here who are barely subsisting on Social Security and also one of the top executives in an auto company. We have people with a high school education and people who have earned doctorates. We have white and black, straight and gay and people with ethnicities from around the world. Of course, God accepts all of us no matter who or where we are—but there are not enough institutions of faith out there with God's level of acceptance.

I became involved in the WISDOM interfaith group of women to have another circle of friends beyond my church and my work as a Realtor. I appreciate that, in this group, people do not try to convert one another. They take acceptance seriously, too.

I'm on the WISDOM board, and my Hindu friend doesn't try to convert me. Our Muslim friend doesn't say to our Hindu friend, "How can you be Hindu? Why don't you consider converting?" None of us evangelizes anyone else.

This behavior allows us to really learn about each other and, after many years working in network news, I can tell you: Americans need to know a whole lot more about the world. I still read The New York Times every day, but the American public's awareness of the larger world is shrinking so fast that many people now think the world can fit into a YouTube screen and a few 140-character Tweets. That lack of awareness is what leads people to slip back into an "Us vs. Them" view of the world. People become polarized. Right now, there are strong signs that we are moving away from acceptance. All of these angry, random, sound bytes surrounding us these days are pushing people toward the extremes. The middle ground of acceptance is vanishing. We all need to work on restoring it.

That's why I appreciate so much the circles of friends in my church and in WISDOM who understand the importance of acceptance.

The only box that's healthy is a box so big that it can hold all of us without anyone ever bumping into a wall.

CHAPTER 44

Anjali Vale
Seeking Common Wavelengths

*I believe that every human is the manifestation
of God, and I bow to that divinity.*

Anjali came to the U.S. with
her new husband when she
was young. Now the parents
of two teenage boys, she and
her husband are comfortably
adapted to life in America. A
working mother and practicing
Hindu, Anjali describes how
her own deep appreciation
for the world's diversity grew
throughout her life—and she
offers hope that the world is,
indeed, catching on to this
important idea.

I MOVED TO the United States from India many years ago with my new husband. We married soon after we first met, and so all at once I had a new land to make my home, a new husband to make my family, and new people to make my friends. Although I was scared and anxious, I was hopeful that, with some work, I would enjoy my new home, family and friends.

Both of my parents, by their behavior, had taught me to have an open mind, to not judge people and to help wherever there is need. They never forced my brother or me to do things or make decisions based on their views, but instead gave us the freedom to choose. My parents always believed in us – believed that we would do the right thing. Their faith in us meant a lot to me.

I always saw my mother, who is a doctor, helping others— even in the middle of the night, if someone came knocking on the door with a pain or wound. I saw her travel extra distances to visit and support patients or friends. My dad is a great philosopher who does a great deal of reading of Indian literature. Now that I am a parent raising my own family and have experienced the world a bit, I feel even closer to my parents, and I appreciate and understand them even more.

Growing up in India, I never felt that faith separated people. India is a diverse country with various languages, castes, and religions. I am Hindu, but my very good friends who helped me grow were of different faiths. After coming to the U.S., I feel strongly that, if your wavelengths match, you can build a strong relationship with any human being, no matter the religion, gender or age of that person.

After finishing my Master of Science in the U.S., I began working as an instructor; it was my first job in my new environment. I still remember that time: My son was just a year old, I had a new job, and I had no family nearby to rely on. It was a time full of anxiety. At work, a colleague who was older and more experienced helped me through that difficult time. Most of my support was coming from a person who was American and of a different race, faith, and nationality. But I don't think we even talked about faith then. She gave me the sense of belonging that I needed.

Similarly, a few other new friends from various backgrounds made me feel at home here.

Raising my children in the States has required me to find a balance in mixing our Indian culture and Hindu faith with our life in America. I teach my sons the pieces that are most important and that they can adapt themselves as Indian-Americans. I hope that, as adults, they will have the best values from both societies.

When I go back to India, to my hometown outside Mumbai, people say, "You are different than before. The U.S. has changed you." I suppose they are right. But I also see a change in the people of India. Life there used to be slow and informal. When I was young, my mother would run an errand and be out for hours, talking to people she ran into along the way. Today, however, people are often in a hurry. Along with a faster pace, people seem to have adopted a more open attitude to the rest of the world. Along with me, India has changed.

Now I have all types of friends from work and the local community, including friends from Ukraine and Japan. We converse about various topics such as the stock market, philosophy or yoga. In India, many faiths coexist peacefully, and I grew up with friends of both genders and of different languages and ethnic backgrounds. I believe every human being is basically the same.

If you have respect and understanding for others, then people will reciprocate the same respect and understanding. People may have different opinions, but if you talk things out with an open mind and try to understand what the other person is thinking, friendship develops. But if people start making assumptions, and no one is paying attention to what the other is thinking, it is very easy to misunderstand each other and lose a friendship over simple things.

Growing up, I was taught the basic values of Hinduism such as respect for other souls, tolerance and pluralism, which for me means that I see all religious paths as equally valid. I am a firm believer that my path is not the only one toward the Supreme God or divinity, but that there may be many true and meaningful paths.

The experiences in my life, with all the people I've met, have taught me to respect other people's races, faiths, nationalities and, most importantly, to simply respect others as human beings. Our outside appearances differ, but, inside, every human being is one and the same.

I believe that every human is the manifestation of God, and I bow to that divinity.

Namaste!

CHAPTER 45

Fran (Shiovitz) Hildebrandt
Crossing Boundaries in Marriage

When you're talking about your spiritual self,
how can you ask someone to compromise?

Fran is a practicing conservative Jew who has honored her interfaith marriage for 35 years. Fran grew up surrounded by neighbors who practiced tolerance and acceptance, despite their cultural and religious differences. That welcoming community, followed by her experience living overseas—and her husband's support of her religious beliefs—all have made Fran who she is today.

AS A CHILD, I had the same kinds of experiences as many non-Christian kids in that era, when schools were not as diverse as they are today. We were expected to participate in Christian holiday activities, such as singing Christmas carols or making Easter eggs. Certainly I recognized that my own religion was being ignored.

But in my neighborhood, there was tolerance and acceptance. Families were friends based on interests and activities. As children, we played with everyone. No distinctions were made by religion. Our parents helped one another, and our friendships were based on our similarities. I saw it as an ideal community. Looking back, I realize that I was given the opportunity to view the world through unbiased eyes—to see people in a positive way.

At the same time, my parents were instilling in my brothers, sister and me a strong sense of identity as Jews and a strong foundation in Judaism.

I was brought up in a conservative Jewish home. My parents kept kosher and observed the holidays. They were active in our synagogue. We attended religious school and synagogue services. But as I got older, I was encouraged to socialize primarily with other Jewish kids. That continued until college, where I met friends who were not Jewish, some of whom are still close friends today. I also met my husband in college.

Certainly my parents would have preferred that I marry someone Jewish, but as it turned out, my parents loved my husband! We connected with each other based on our similarities, and not our differences. Yet because of my husband's beliefs he did not feel slighted or disrespected by my faith. We waited six years to get married, until we worked everything out, although I don't think we'll ever work out all of the quirks.

It's hard to combine faiths on a daily basis. We maintain a Jewish home in which we keep kosher and observe the holidays. (Our friends and family are both amused and amazed at how well my husband can conduct a seder.) I am active in my synagogue. My husband attends services and synagogue functions with me. He maintains his own beliefs but is able to integrate them with my practice of Judaism. We have tried to have a marriage that is based on love and mutual respect for each other's beliefs. I give my husband a lot of credit, because he has had to make more compromises than I have.

According to Jewish law, a child born of a Jewish woman or convert to Judaism is Jewish. At the beginning of our marriage, we agreed that our children would be raised Jewishly. We would actively help each of them to develop a strong Jewish identity that would be religious, cultural, and social. We kept this promise.

Since we did not have a Christmas tree in our home, our family spent Christmas with my husband's parents. The boys understood that Christmas was not their holiday—that it was Grandpa's and Grandma's holiday—but they were allowed to enjoy it, as Jews, and not feel guilty. Easter often falls right during Passover, so we handled it differently as the boys got older. Sometimes I would bring kosher-for-Passover food with me to serve at my husband's parents' home. Other times they came to our home on Passover and I would serve a Kosher for Passover Easter dinner. Both sets of grandparents were friendly toward each other, so we were able to spend birthdays and Mother's Day and Father's Day together.

I'm not a proponent of mixed marriages. At its best, marriage is difficult. There are always problems and conflicts, and based on today's statistics, not many people seem willing or able to resolve the tough issues couples face. When the partners in a marriage practice two different religions, life is even more complicated. When you're talking about your spiritual self, how can you ask someone to compromise?

For those considering an interfaith marriage, I would recommend you do the following: Attend services of the other person's faith and participate in family holidays–see if each of you can feel comfortable doing this. I also recommend taking a class that presents an objective point of view of the religion of your partner. It's another opportunity to learn if you could be comfortable being part of someone else's faith. And finally, talk to couples (as in more than one) in interfaith marriages. Learn firsthand some of the joys and pitfalls that a mixed marriage creates.

Having an interfaith marriage has given my sons a different perspective on spirituality and diversity. They have much more respect and appreciation for various spiritual and cultural traditions. My sons have had opportunities to see religion function at its best and also the way it can create suspicion and separation. Our family experiences have taught them the importance of communication combined with love and respect.

Living overseas also shaped who I am today. My husband and I, along with our two oldest sons, lived in Medan, N. Sumatra, Indonesia for two years. We lived and taught in a Muslim community. This was an amazing chance to experience other cultures and, as a Jew, it was especially gratifying to feel accepted by such a diverse religious community as existed in Medan. Today I teach high school English in a very non-Jewish community; I don't know if I could do this so successfully without the childhood and life experiences I've had. My husband is a remarkable man who has taught me a lot. Even after all these years, there are still new questions about Judaism that arise. When that happens, it is often because my husband will ask why I want to do something. Sometimes I have to re-learn it to explain it. More importantly, it forces me to analyze, "Why *do* I do this? Why *is* this important to me?" Sometimes I have taken rituals for granted.

One of the benefits of having a husband like mine is having a partner who respects and honors Judaism. The more I'm around people who are not Jewish, the more it makes me appreciate my own religion. We've been married for 35 years – together for 41 years – and my husband has really helped to make me a better Jew.

CHAPTER 46

Stephanie Fenton
A Higher Calling in Marriage

Why do some marriages fall apart while others last for life?

Stephanie Fenton is a journalist and photographer best known for her long-running series of columns called Holidays & Festivals. Over the past decade as other newspapers and magazines have cut back on staffing, Stephanie has emerged as the only American journalist whose exclusive focus is weekly news coverage of these religious  and cultural milestones. Her regular readers live in countries as far flung as China and New Zealand, South Africa and Canada. In this story, Stephanie focuses on differing customs of marriage around the world—and the universal values that can inspire deep friendship.

THROUGH MY WORK, I have had the absolute pleasure of meeting men and women of almost every religion. These individuals have inspired me, changed me and opened my eyes to the beauty of our colorful world. But this story focuses on a remarkable series of experiences shared by my husband, Kevin, and a group of Hindu young men he worked with during a graduate-level class. All of these men were from India and were planning to have arranged marriages.

After each day of his field work for this class, my husband would excitedly tell me about his talks concerning marriage with the group of Hindu young men and one man, in particular, whom he had been assigned to work with. In spite of their vastly different cultures, this Hindu man's view of marriage was refreshing and ultimately matched so many of his own ideals, my husband said.

This encounter was especially meaningful to both of us as our 10-year wedding anniversary approaches. Kevin and I find we are talking a lot about the course of our marriage. Have our outlooks changed since we were first married? Of course, this brings up the related question: Why do some marriages fall apart while others last for life?

This field work was part of Kevin's graduate studies in historic preservation at a local university. In this phase of his program, he had the opportunity to be part of a hands-on field school with a small group of about 25 students. Most of the students were studying preservation, with four or five of them drawn from a construction management program. When the group was split into teams, Kevin was put on a team with the students from that management program; all of those students were from India. Over a week, Kevin worked with these men on restoring an historic building.

As they worked together, they talked about many things, but one subject that continued to come up was marriage. Kevin was the only married man on the team—but he quickly learned that all of his other new friends were planning to marry. In fact, they were looking forward to arranged marriages. That was quite a cultural difference for Kevin!

Kevin told me: "I was surprised that all of them seemed very confident about the idea of arranged marriage, as if it was something they had always expected would be a part of their lives. One student, named Mahipal, stood out to me when this subject came up in conversation. What made Mahipal different is that, when we spoke about the future, the other students were planning to start a career that likely would keep them in the United States. That was not Mahipal's plan. He was very certain he would be going back home to India to be married and live there."

Kevin was surprised by Mahipal's plans and asked him, "Why not stay here with the others? Why move back to India?"

Mahipal grinned and said simply, "It's home, man! It's who I am." If he did not return home, Mahipal told Kevin, then he feared that much of his life would vanish. His own children would grow up differently than he had. A valuable generational chain would be broken in his family.

Kevin told me: "There was real passion in his eyes as he talked about this. Listening to him describe his home and his family and his culture, I was moved. He was clearly concerned with far more than his own life, his own desires. He wanted to live in such a way that he could help to preserve his larger family, his faith and his culture."

Mahipal also was unique in this group, because he already knew his bride and was planning to marry her upon his return to India. For him, this was not abstract speculation about marriage. He was making concrete plans. And, he was excited about what lay ahead for him.

Kevin asked: "Are you afraid it might not work out? Are you afraid you might wind up feeling unhappy?"

At that point, Mahipal stopped what he was doing, sat down on the scaffolding high above the ground, and said, "Listen, our customs have been in place for a very long time because this system works. Both of us have decided to follow this custom, because we have seen so many positive examples. When two people in my culture decide to get married, it works because we take pride in entering into this agreement. Both of our families are invested in this. Marriage is not just about your own desires as an individual."

As Kevin told me this story, he paused. Then, he told me, "It was at that moment I realized my new Hindu friend and I were not so different. Our marriages are based on similar principles. Marriage should not be about a selfish search for happiness. Marriage is about our role in a larger family—our success as a good spouse and parent. That's what defines 'a good life.' Mahipal and I both agreed that, arranged or not, the goals we set for ourselves in marriage are the same."

One day, when Kevin and Mahipal were removing some windows together, they had another chance to converse.

"What challenges do you face in your marriage?" he asked Kevin.

Kevin told his friend, "Once you're married, you no longer face challenges alone; you have a partner to face everything with that arises with you."

"I think the bond in marriage can run as deep as we choose to make it," Mahipal said. "It seems that all of the effort, love, patience and sacrifice you put into marriage is what ultimately makes the relationship so beautiful and the bond so strong."

"Life's about the difference we make in the lives of those around us," Kevin told him.

I was so moved by Kevin's story about his new friend that it deepened my own sense of marriage and family commitment. I was so pleased to hear about this unexpected new friendship! And it surprised me to learn that a group of guys laboring at a work site wound up sharing such inspiring thoughts with each other!

"Wow," I said to Kevin. "I want to share your story. It's remarkable. By telling me, you know, it's now my story, too. And, I want to share this with others through the pages of this new book. Who knows who else might be touched by your story?"

He nodded. The look I saw in his eyes was the look of an inspired man. "To be inspired by a friend who seemed, at first, so different—is such a gift," he said. "We need friends to remind us to be our best selves."

CHAPTER 47

Shahina Begg
Reaching Out, Generation to Generation

As I set off on this long journey, I had no idea how the meeting with Victor's parents would go.

Shahina is a co-founder of WISDOM, so she also is part of this book's opening chapter, in which she talks about organizing this diverse network of women. Within her own family, Shahina is part of a remarkable multi-generational tradition of crossing boundaries in friendship. Born and raised in Hinduism, she converted to Islam as an adult. After reading Shahina's story here, you will meet Shahina's daughter in the next chapter.

THIS IS THE story of how I first met one of my best friends in life—and it was not at all what I expected when I set out on this long journey.

I was born into a Brahmin-class family in Hinduism. Of course, the caste system is not as important as it once was, but our culture and our Hindu traditions were important to my family. We did not go to the temple frequently, but we always visited the temple for special occasions. To this day, when my siblings visit my mother near Goa, in western India, she takes them to the temple. Because I converted to Islam, I no longer go to the temple like they do—but I always make sure that my mother is able to visit a temple here in the U.S., when she comes to see us.

My own interfaith journey began in my childhood and has extended through my entire life. I grew up in Bombay, now Mumbai, which is a very cosmopolitan city; I had friends of different faiths as I was growing up. Dad was the assistant commissioner of police for Bombay and Mom was a homemaker.

I came to America in 1973 and began working on a master's in business administration in January of 1974. That's when I first met my husband, Victor, who was studying business as well. I was 20 and Victor was a little older. About a year and a half later, we got married. When I first came to America, I wasn't sure if I was going to stay here for good—but meeting Victor made the difference.

My dad was very open-minded when he heard the news. At first—as many Indian families do—he wanted to check on Victor's family. He was very busy with his police work at the time, so at first he sent one of his officers over from Bombay to Hyderabad, where Victor's family lived. However, this officer came back and said: "There's some problem with the family address. I can't find the place."

Dad asked me about this, and I said, "There must be some mistake."

Finally, my father himself went to Hyderabad. He met Victor's family and he said to me, "Victor has a very good family. Now, I'm going to give my blessing for your marriage."

The one piece of advice Dad gave me was: "Don't think of moving back and settling in India again. The society here still is not ready to let you live happily here. Make your life in America after this."

So, even as we were preparing to get married, there was some anxiety back home about the different backgrounds of our families. When we got married here, we actually celebrated these differences and it became quite an exceptional gathering of people in 1975. We had our civil ceremony at the Oak Park City Hall, near where I lived at the time. This little city just north of Detroit still has a large Jewish population. As we arranged to get married, the mayor of Oak Park became quite intrigued with the whole idea. I was from a Hindu family and was getting married to a Muslim in a ceremony performed by this mayor, who was Jewish. The mayor was so fascinated by our story that he presented Dad with a key to the city of Oak Park.

At that time, Victor's parents were not able to come for the marriage. And, soon, Victor and I moved to Canada for a few years to complete our studies and to work in the Toronto area. I had converted to Islam just before we got married, but at that time neither Victor nor I were as involved as we are today in Muslim traditions.

This more casual approach to our religious traditions eventually led to some anxiety, when I made my first trip back to India to see my family and to meet Victor's parents. Because of our schedules, Victor couldn't get away for as much time as I planned to spend—a couple of months. This was a very important trip. After living in the Toronto area for about five years, Victor and I were about to immigrate back to America and to settle permanently in the U.S. In January of 1979, our first child, Sami, was born and, by early 1980, we wanted the family back in India to have a chance to see little Sami. As it turned out, Sami celebrated his 1st birthday in India.

As I set off on this long journey, I had no idea how the meeting with Victor's parents would go. His mother's name was Hasina Sultana, and his family was very well-known in their region of central India. Victor's grandfather was chief justice of the Hyderabad court and his uncles also were justices.

I had not studied much about Islam, at that point. I did not cover my hair like I do now. I didn't even know all of the Arabic prayers that are important in Islam. What would Victor's parents think about me? I heard the old jokes about problems with "in-laws" and I began to worry. This new relationship was going to be even more complex in my case.. I was coming from another faith and I knew that Victor's mother was very religious.

My first stop in India was Bombay, where I stayed with my family for a couple of weeks. Then, my parents made the train trip with Sami and me to Hyderabad—a journey of about eight hours. We rode on the old-style trains, in which the compartment doors opened right onto the platform.

As the miles passed, I did get a little bit scared about what would be awaiting us when we arrived. I was wearing loose Indian clothing, which was appropriate, but the type of scarf I was wearing did not completely cover my hair in the Muslim style.

When we finally arrived at the station, we had not even left the train when one of Victor's younger sisters showed up at the door of our compartment. She had come to look me over. But as she reached out to hug me, I could feel the strength and the warmth in that hug. I could feel her love reaching out to me. Then, she said, "You look nice! And, there's nothing to worry about. Mummie will love you. She is looking forward to seeing you."

Still, I wondered what would happen. We stepped out of the train, and everything was so loud on the platform! Many Indians travel by train, and the crowd was rushing in all directions. Porters were shouting. I put Sami into his stroller to make it easier to walk through all the people.

Where was Victor's family in that big crowd? I could not see them at first. And how should I greet them? In Hindu custom, we kneeled down and touched an elder's feet out of respect, but this was not the case in Islam, I knew. In Islam, the only one you kneel to is Allah, and you show affection for other people with an embrace. Would I get this right?

Then, I saw through the crowd these people with flowers—a huge garland of white jasmine and roses. It was my mother-in-law, my father-in-law, another sister-in-law and her husband and kids. They all were waiting to greet me with these flowers, which they placed around my neck. This was such a warm welcome full of embraces.

Our entire time in Hyderabad was wonderful! I knew very little about Muslim prayers and my mother-in-law brought in a teacher each day, so I remember that time, as well, because it's when I learned a great deal about the basics of prayer in Islam. Victor's mother was a petite lady with nice features and a particular way of carrying herself, so that you could tell she came from a noble family. She liked to wear a sari and sometimes wore flowers in her hair.

Later, she came to live with us in our home in America for 12 years, before she passed away in 1994—and she became one of my best friends. It was so easy to love her. She did things like quietly praise me to other people, when I wasn't around. I first heard about this from friends who would tell me what she had said. That surprised me, at first. But it taught me that all those old stereotypes about "in-laws" were totally false—at least in my family. I was blessed to have those years with her.

Here's another example: At first, I wasn't a good cook—at least not in the Hyderabadi style of cooking—but she was such a good teacher. I cannot recall her ever criticizing me. At first, she would cook things herself and show me what she was doing. As she got older, she would sit with me in the kitchen as I cooked. When the food was done, she only ever said good things about the dishes.

She had one specific spot in our family room—her chair, where she would settle in each day and begin her routine. She loved soap operas on television and she also loved to pray with beads, chanting the names of God with the beads. She also would turn on an audio player near her chair to help with the chanting. All three things were going on at the same time: soap operas, the beads and the audio for the chanting. She loved it.

And I loved her. Sometimes I think about that train ride across India as I wondered what she would be like. As I wondered: Would she accept me?

As it turned out, our family was blessed. And, most importantly, so much of what she did in our friendship was quietly done. She always used to say to me: "Whatever good you do for others, never boast of it. If you do, your goodness will be washed away. Whatever good you can do in life for someone else—do it quietly and with the full intention of your heart."

CHAPTER 48

Sofia B. Latif
Balancing Faith and Family

Sometimes my father and my mother's uncle would debate some of the teachings—the way that I imagine other families debate politics—but then they would sit down and have dinner together.

Sofia is a practicing Muslim whose life has been influenced by the differing religious backgrounds of her parents. Her mother is Shahina Begg, who tells her story in the previous chapter. Sofia attributes her commitment to issues of unity and diversity to the example her parents set throughout her childhood.

THROUGHOUT MY LIFE, my parents taught me to build relationships based upon the values that I share with others. Through their example, I learned to move beyond just tolerance for religious diversity—to actually love and embrace people of all faiths.

My parents met in college in the United States, although they are both Indian immigrants. My mother is from Bombay and was raised Hindu, and my father is from a Muslim family from Hyderabad. When they married, my mother decided to convert to Islam, and when my brothers and I were born, we were raised Muslim.

From a very young age, I remember learning to read the Qur'an from my father's mother. I attended Sunday School at the mosque, prayed five times a day alongside my parents, and fasted during the month of Ramadan. Islam was a central part of my life, and I was very proud to be Muslim. But unlike many of my Sunday School friends, there was a large part of my life that did not revolve around Islam.

Often during school breaks, my family would travel to visit my mother's relatives. My Hindu cousins sometimes spent entire summers at our home and, during weddings and other big celebrations, both sides of my family would come together. During these times, my parents fostered a welcoming environment where the tensions often associated with differing cultures and traditions could not be felt. Sometimes my father and my mother's uncle would talk and even debate about religious teachings—the way that I imagine other families debate about politics—but then they would sit down and have dinner together. Both my father and mother's uncle are devout followers of their separate faiths, but they did not allow the differences in their religious beliefs to interfere with family relationships.

Reflecting now, I realize how my parents—despite the challenges brought by religious diversity—prioritized the values of hospitality, of respect to elders and of family. My brothers and I were not taught to see the lines that religion often places between people, but rather, we were shown how to love and admire the humanity that unifies them.

Sofia B. Latif • 247

When I joined the sixth grade at a public middle school, I decided to begin wearing the traditional Muslim headscarf, knowing that I would be the only one to do so. It was a difficult transition, but even at such a young age, I was firm in my faith and confident that when others began to know me, they would accept me for who I was. My parents' example, in so many subtle and obvious ways, had given me proof that people who ultimately shared the same values would find friendship and amity. My best friends throughout my middle and high school years were Shannon Fink, a Jew, and Alka Tandon, a Hindu.

Today, I recognize that my passion for working toward creating pluralistic societies with religious and cultural understanding is a direct result of my upbringing. During my senior year in high school, when I heard about the *Children of Abraham Project*, I was truly excited to get involved. This was an opportunity to work with young adults from over a dozen different racial, cultural, socioeconomic and religious backgrounds to tell a common story—the story of how Abraham's two sons, Isaac and Ishmael, the patriarchs of two great religions, came together upon their father's death to bury him. The goal was to use this story as an example for how our communities today can overcome the hate and fear that divides us. As I worked with this diverse group on developing the storyline for the play, I once again found myself searching for the values that connected us and brought us together. It was only after we, as a group, were able to overcome the tensions of diversity, that we could co-create what has now become an award-winning production and documentary that has traveled across the U.S. and Jerusalem.

CHAPTER 49

Rabbi Dorit Edut
From One Diverse Community to Another

I realized that this felt a lot like what I experienced in relationships I had formed, years ago, in elementary school and scouting.

For more than 40 years, Rabbi Edut has been a Jewish educator in metro Detroit. She was ordained in 2006 and has served synagogues in New York and Michigan. While working in Detroit, she helped organize the Detroit Interfaith Outreach Network (DION), where many groups come together to share in projects that revitalize the city through a focus on youth. The group has organized programs for career exploration, conflict resolution and cultural  awareness. In April 2015, Rabbi Dorit helped create the Greater Detroit Muslim-Jewish Solidarity Council to encourage social action and cultural exchanges to strengthen the relationships between these two communities. She strongly believes in the power of interfaith work to bring peace and enlightenment into our modern world.

AS A FIRST-GENERATION American, I grew up feeling a little bit "new" here without fully understanding what prejudices there might be in this society. Maybe it was because my first languages were French and German, which my parents spoke with me, and I learned English later from playing with the other kids in our neighborhood. Maybe it was because my parents, who had come from Germany and Luxembourg, always expressed their deep gratitude to this country that offered them a refuge and a place to begin life anew after each somehow had survived the Nazi Holocaust. Maybe it was because I also observed my parents interacting with people from many different backgrounds: our Italian produce man, our Irish mailman, our African-American housekeeper. My parents always treated them as friends. I saw my parents' many acts of kindness attempting to cheer up or help out these friends in some way.

When I went to MacDowell Elementary School, my first friends were African-American twins whose mother was the crossing guard and later became our Girl Scout leader. The neighborhood I grew up in was 60 percent Jewish, 35 percent African-American Baptist and 5 percent Caucasian Protestant. We formed some close relationships through scouts where we camped, traveled to interesting sites all over Detroit and Michigan, and even attended some worship services and holidays together at one another's churches or synagogues.

But there were some teachers at our school who were openly prejudiced: Whenever there was any disturbance in class, an African-American kid usually was singled out, even though he or she may have been innocent. I am ashamed to say that I did not speak out then on behalf of my classmates, nor did any of my other Jewish friends, because we had been taught to obey our teachers and not question authority. I only began to question this concept when I got to high school and the civil rights movement was at its peak.

One day I had my own encounter with prejudice when the two boys who lived across our backyard fence and attended a Catholic school started taunting my sister and me: "You Jews are Christ-killers and will burn in hell! You can't hide your horns from us!" While I didn't totally understand what they were saying, I was hurt enough to report it to my father, who went and had a talk with the boys' father. I don't think that conversation went well, because after that we never had anything more to do with those boys or their parents. My father let the bushes along the fence grow tall, blocking our view of their house.

Yet this experience was counterbalanced by the many positive experiences we had with other Christian people—such as the woman who was my father's nanny in Berlin who always sent us marzipan and lebkuchen at Christmastime. She seemed overjoyed to meet my sister and me when we visited Europe as children with our parents. It was then, too, that my parents took us into the awe-inspiring cathedrals in France and Italy to experience their beauty and the gorgeous artwork by the great masters. I learned all about Christianity this way and could not help but be moved by the suffering, sorrow and compassion that were expressed so exquisitely. My mother, too, told us of having to pretend she was Catholic during the war when she was in hiding in Southern France, and of the selfless acts of bravery of those in the French Underground who cared for her, saving her and my grandparents.

Beyond these cross-cultural experiences, I had a strong Jewish upbringing as well, attending Hebrew school all the way through the high school years, in part because I was eager to speak Hebrew and also because I loved Jewish history, the Bible and the holidays and customs. At home, we celebrated all the holidays; and sometimes I went to Sabbath services by myself, as I began to feel a deep spiritual connection to God.

When I was 13, I asked about becoming a rabbi, but was told by my rabbi, "No, honey, but you can marry one!" That felt like a knife going through me and somehow I knew I would have to wait until the right time came along. So, I became a teacher, and later, a family and crisis counselor. Then, finally, I was ordained as a rabbi at age 56.

While I had originally envisioned myself as a pulpit rabbi, this was not my ultimate path. While working with the newly invigorated Isaac Agree Downtown Synagogue in Detroit—the only standing synagogue left within the city limits—I began reaching out to other nearby clergy to see how we might come together to support the work of transforming this great city. Many of the issues facing Detroit seemed at their essence to be spiritual ones and I knew that the faith community had always worked hard to help the people of Detroit when government and other institutions had either failed them or not provided adequate support.

In a very short time, I got to know many religious leaders from many faiths and denominations. Together we formed a networking organization that lifts up the families and children of Detroit, creating ways of bringing the resources of our different congregations together for this purpose.

As we engaged in this work, we discovered something else. By sharing in these projects, we were getting to know each other and forming strong friendships. I realized that this felt a lot like what I experienced in relationships I had formed, years ago, in elementary school and scouting. Through the years, we have learned about differences and similarities in our faiths and this understanding has helped us deepen our appreciation of each other and of the awesomeness of God, our creator.

One of the lasting images from these experiences occurred at our first interfaith service. There I was: a Jewish woman rabbi, sitting at the altar of a Catholic church. First, we listened to a young Muslim boy recite verses of the Qur'an, then to drummers praising the divine in the form of Krishna and finally to a rousing praise chant from the congregation of men, women and children from many traditions.

"This is what God wants to see in the world," a voice inside me said. "All of us together—praying in peace and love!"

CHAPTER 50

Serene K. Zeni
Differences Can Strengthen Friendships

Labels conceal our life stories ... Rather than clarifying, they often blind us to wonderful people we encounter in our lives.

Serene K. Zeni is a health care attorney and a mother raising four children. She has served on numerous nonprofit boards as part of her strong commitment to community service and interfaith outreach. Drawing on those experiences, she writes here about the many ways common stereotypes become barriers to friendship.

DO YOU REMEMBER going to the grocery store with your parents to pick out a box of cereal for the toy you had to have, not caring whether you actually liked the cereal? Do you remember going to a Kmart a week after school started to pick out the latest Trapper Keeper and wrapping your textbooks with paper you would spend the rest of the year decorating?

I loved coming home after school as a child, when my brothers and I would sit around the television set together to watch the newest cartoon, starting with "He-Man" from my earliest memories to "Animaniacs" in my later ones. Some of my favorite childhood memories involved my family waiting anxiously for the "Alf" theme song on TV so we could say at the dark screen sprinkled with what appeared to be stars, "It's not space!" Then, Alf would remove the camera lens cover. I will never forget cheering on "The Bad Boys" of the Detroit Pistons when the Los Angeles Lakers won in the final minutes of the NBA Finals in 1988.

The nostalgia of my childhood is classic Americana—but you might never guess that if I introduced myself to you as a Muslim woman born to Syrian immigrants.

Now more than ever, labels conceal our life stories. If you meet me with the label of "Muslim," then you may wonder: How can I be a devout adherent to the faith of "those" people and, at the same time, stake my claim as a true-blooded American, through and through?

The challenge of living as an American Muslim does not lie in practicing the faith. In fact, I tell people that America actually preserved my Islam and has strengthened my faith. Had my parents not brought me to this "land of the free and the home of the brave," the practice of my faith would have been confined by the dictatorial regime of Hafez al-Assad, which strangled the light of Islam at every possible opportunity. My father's birth city of Hama was terrorized by al-Assad in the 1982 Hama massacre, and my mother's birth province now suffers the same terror under the hands of his son.

America gave my parents the freedom to teach me Islam as it was intended by God, or Allah, as we say in Arabic. The liberating inclusiveness in American society allowed my parents to give us the bounty of knowing people of all faiths and loving them as brothers and sisters, as God taught us to love in the Qur'an. The absence of shackles imposed by a ruthless regime opened the doors for my parents to give us a complete picture of our beloved Prophet Muhammad (peace and blessings be upon him), whose name and teachings had been deliberately and methodically tarnished in a country whose government feared the influence of a kind, tolerant, and merciful way of life.

Indeed, it is because of America that I love and adore Islam. It is also because of Islam that I adore America. I express my gratitude to God every day for giving me the honor of being American and allowing me to raise my American children in a country that upholds the very values at the core of Islam, like no other country in this world.

In America, a little Muslim girl could grow up across the street from a devout Jewish family and love them as her own. Mrs. Peterman may or may not remember me, but I will forever be indebted to her for watching me after school countless times when my mother was attending dental school an hour away from home and my father was late returning from work.

I try to imagine a place outside of America where a little girl can experience the bounties of diversity the way I have. As an awkward sixth grader, I could not have been more grateful to be paired up with my friend Priya, who helped me fly with ease through what was shaping up as the most difficult year of my life socially. I will never forget my dear friends Debbie and Kim, each of whom invited me to their Bat Mitzvahs when I really wasn't the coolest kid to invite to such an event. In high school, my friends and I reveled in the fact that our lunch table was comprised of black, white, English, French, Indian and Arabic girls.

God has showered me with a diverse circle of people who have propelled me forward throughout my career. Michigan Attorney General Mike Cox gave me my first job, despite the scarf on my head that deterred countless other employers from hiring an otherwise successful law student. Every day I think of my colleague and mentor, Jack, who would take time out of his busy day in my first few years at the attorney general's office to listen to my far-reaching legal arguments. Jack would give me valuable perspective, while teaching me Hebrew words and comparing them to Arabic ones. My direct supervisor, Tom, spent a great deal of his free time volunteering for his church or running in a marathon to support community organizations. He also would open doors of opportunity for me, despite pushback from more senior attorneys.

My dearest friends since leaving the attorney general's office are my former supervisors, Merry and Amy, who always responded to my ambitious requests with support, pushing me to achieve what no one could have expected in their first three years as an attorney. My first job in a "big law firm" was given to me by a man whose life also revolves around his Church, family and values—and who saw me beyond the scarf I wore.

What I have learned through these many friendships is that, when we first encounter people, we have to look beyond the surface. Our tendency is to quickly notice details and to distill them into labels. But labels are not helpful. Rather than clarifying, they often blind us to wonderful people we encounter in our lives.

We all tend to think of our own interests first. When a friend encouraged me to serve on the board of WISDOM, I saw the opportunity as one that would enable me to educate others about Islam and Muslims. I never imagined I would be the one to gain the education—until the day I sat on a panel for WISDOM's extraordinary program Five Women, Five Journeys. On my panel, there were Jewish, Christian, Hindu and Baháʼí women beside me. At that time, I still covered my hair. The rest of the panel looked much like the audience in front of us, with the exception of the Hindu woman dressed in traditional Indian clothing. From my perspective, I was the most different and had the most to teach because Islam and Muslims were the most harshly treated in society.

As I listened to their stories, these women gave me the greatest education of my life on how wrong my perspective was. Every one of these women was like me! Every woman on the panel had been isolated—reduced unfairly to a label at some point in her life. Every woman's faith had been unfairly scrutinized or mis-characterized—in some cases even more than I had experienced as a Muslim. Every woman had faced challenges, had worked hard to gain acceptance and educate the society around her about her faith, her community and her culture. Every woman had been undermined and hijacked by stereotypes.

I had been assuming that my pathway to improved relationships in the larger community lay in convincing people of my American identity. What I learned from this group of women is that I am American—*because I am different*. We are a nation of immigrants. We all have struggled with perceptions.

In college, I was an avid student of American political theory and particularly came to appreciate Thomas Jefferson. As my eyes opened, I thought again about his statement: "I never considered a difference of opinion in politics, in religion, in philosophy, as cause for withdrawing from a friend."

Finally, I could see what he meant: If we begin to draw lines between friendship and faith, we do so at the risk of losing our identity as Americans.

CHAPTER 51

The Rev. Megan Walther
In Friendship, Our Journeys Connect

Our fears were compounded by the anxiety of not being able to reach our friends. Were they worried? Were we near them—or increasingly farther and farther away?

The Rev. Megan Walther is a pastor at Clarkston United Methodist Church in Michigan. She believes that making a friend is making a commitment. So, she encourages people to nurture friendships intentionally, including making time and truly caring for each other. Like the previous story in this book, Megan has discovered that the world can become a more compassionate and welcoming place through such relationships. In her story, she describes one such moment of revelation.

WHILE MY HUSBAND, Joel, and I were in seminary, we met men and women from around the world. Even though we all were Christians in our seminary, there were enormous cultural differences between us. Many branches of Christianity were represented within our seminary community in Washington, D.C. and we quickly learned that within our shared faith, there were many ethnic, regional and denominational barriers.

Peter-Pal and Agnes are one couple we befriended from a small town in the Great Hungarian Plain east of Budapest. Our first conversations involved food. For example, they observed, "American bread is too sweet." So, Joel, who loves to bake, made them a loaf of bread without added sugar. Food became a connection between us. In their tradition, as in many cultures around the world, friends shared food preparation as a communal experience. We bonded over meals, both before, during and after the food was consumed.

What divided us was theology. We came from different branches of Christianity with important differences separating us. During those long meals, we often fell into spirited debates over matters of faith. That led to other debates as our theological conversations revealed we had varying assumptions about social issues. Even though we all were seminarians in a Protestant Christian school, many barriers still separated us.

Grace and compassion deepened our friendship. Even though we disagreed on many very important points of belief, we agreed that we all are called to love and compassion and that we could form a strong foundation as friends,

Friendship triumphed to such an extent that, after graduation and assignments as pastors—Joel and I in Michigan and Peter-Pal and Agnes back in Hungary—we agreed to intentionally make occasional visits back and forth. As pastors living on modest budgets, this was an epic undertaking involving the cost of international travel, plus planning for planes, trains and automobiles. A year after graduation, they came to visit us in Michigan. Two years after graduation came our turn to visit them in Hungary.

While both Joel and I are experienced travelers, our foray into Eastern Europe carried us through regions where no English was spoken or appeared on signs. Landing in Budapest, we knew that we had to take trains for several hours to their town, involving at least one transfer along the way. At the airport, we gathered up our bags and hopped on a bus to the Budapest train station. Confident that this would be an easy matter of finding the right train, then making our transfer at the correct midpoint, we settled into our seats and watched the landscape pass.

The first sign of trouble was an unexpected stop with no station in sight. We simply sat and waited for nearly an hour before the train began to crawl forward. Next, we stopped at small station and a woman in uniform strode through the cars, calling out an obviously important message in Hungarian.

We had no clue what she was trying to convey—but all the other passengers stood up, gathered their bags and left the train. Joel and I looked at each other in confusion and followed the crowd onto the tiny platform. People overwhelmed the depot. Some stood chatting with friends; some sat down as if settling in for a long wait; some got on buses. But not a soul spoke English in this little town. We tried to engage one passenger after another. We were unsure whether another train was coming. We had no idea where the buses were going. There was no telephone in the depot and, as experienced international travelers, we had left our American cell phones at home.

An hour passed. Then another. After several hours, another train pulled into the station and the families still seated in the depot jammed onto the train. We weren't sure what to do. Joel and I pulled out our original train tickets bearing the name of our anticipated point of transfer. We accosted the train's conductor, waving our tickets, pointing at the town printed there, repeating that one location over and over.

The conductor looked at us in puzzlement. He could tell we were lost. He was honestly trying to answer our query, but his response was not obvious to us. He was shrugging as he motioned and spoke in Hungarian—conveying that we should board this train. We thought it was heading to our destination.

We soon learned that he was conveying something different: Boarding this train eventually would move us in the right direction. We got on board.

At this point, I needed to calm my husband, who usually is confident in such situations. This time, he was not. An awareness was growing between us that we were nearly 5,000 miles from home in a land where we could understand nothing that was printed or spoken around us; our handy smartphones were missing and our friends were unable to help us. We felt alone. The cultural chasms around us deepened.

As we rode, we kept listening for announcements and watching for signs—trying to find the transfer location listed on our tickets. We never found it! Instead, the train simply stopped, everyone got off and the conductor made it clear that we had to disembark, as well. We walked into a gray, Communist-era town of concrete with a gritty feel that anyone who is familiar with pre-1990 Eastern Europe will be able to envision. Now, we were several hours beyond our original arrival time at our friends' town! And now, we were deeper into non-English-speaking Eastern Europe than we had ever expected on this fondly anticipated vacation. Our fears were compounded by the anxiety of not being able to reach our friends. Were they worried? Were we near them—or increasingly farther and farther away?

Finally, at the station, we were able to find a railroad employee who spoke English and agreed to help us sort out the schedules! She explained that we were nowhere near the original transfer point printed on our tickets. However, she helped us find a schedule for a train that would take us to our final destination— our friends' hometown. Half an hour later, that train arrived, we made the transfer and rode another hour to the town where our friends were waiting.

Our fears were high, but our friends greeted us with such open arms and gifts of water and food that we quickly recalled the foundations of our friendship. How chilling it had been to experience that disorientation, that isolation, while riding on trains with no clear destination! How warm it was to find our friends waiting patiently through the hours-long delays, bearing wonderful snacks and loving expressions.

Eventually we learned: When it became clear that we were delayed, they and their family members guessed that an unexpected turn had sent us into disorienting territory. They had no idea where we were but they began reaching out.

"My father got on the telephone and called the central Hungarian train station. He sent out a regional alert for 'two lost Americans' bearing your description," Peter-Pal told us.

For hours, as we rode trains or sat in stations, our anxiety rising at the ever-grayer and ever-more-foreign landscape around us, an entire family had been fanning out looking for us—alerting others in stations across Hungary. We had not even hoped for such a response. And while we managed to find our own way to their town, our friendship was renewed in a powerful way to learn that—even while we were lost, they were reaching out with nationwide appeals, trying to bring us home.

CHAPTER 52

Najah Bazzy
Our Hands Reach Out

God wants us to see other people beyond all of the distinctions that can so easily distract us. God wants us to see each other's souls.

Najah Bazzy is an internationally known expert on trans-cultural issues in health care. As a pioneer in this professional field, she has contributed to conferences, training and new policies on nursing, medical ethics and related issues. She also is founder and executive director of Zaman International, a nonprofit focused on empowering vulnerable women and children in marginalized communities. By 2017, Zaman was working in 14 countries and had touched the lives of more than 1.3 million people.

I NO LONGER see the outside differences in the people I meet. I see people's souls before I see their faces. I believe this way of seeing the world is a gift from God.

Much of my perspective on the world was shaped by my childhood in Dearborn, Michigan. At the time, our neighborhood was a "United Nations" of immigrant families who all shared similar stories. We simply assumed it was common for some of our friends to attend Catholic catechism or become altar servers, while others studied Arabic and the Qur'an at a mosque. A major influence on my early life was my aunt, who used to help with the burial customs in our community, including washing the dead. At age 15, she taught me how to perform a proper washing following our Muslim customs. Preparing a body for burial is such a profound experience that I grew up seeing the universal commonalities we all share as human beings. Grief crosses all cultures and boundaries. Then, as a nurse, I helped to deliver babies. My hands touched so many people at the beginning and end of life that my vision has forever changed as I encounter new people—whether in a meeting, in a line at the grocery store or in the seats of an airplane.

Just before we all celebrated the Fourth of July in 2016, we were thrilled that one of our young relatives Mohamed Bazzi was able to come home for a visit. I could describe how he is related to me, but we don't dwell on such distinctions in Arab-American families. He was 21, a bright young man with wonderful career prospects studying business at Northeastern University in Boston. We rarely got to see him, so the whole family was excited that he had come home for a visit.

This was near the end of the fasting month of Ramadan, a time when Muslim families always try to gather. Plus, his sister had just had a baby. Mohamed was eager to see them. He arrived at the apartment where his mother and his two sisters were staying; he spent time with them. But, it seemed like such a brief visit that summer. All too soon, he was on his way back to the airport. His mother urged him to stay through the entire Fourth holiday, but Mohamed was the kind of young man who was always organizing activities to make other students feel welcome in the

Boston area. Because the feast at the end of Ramadan that year coincided with the national holiday, he had organized a barbecue for an international group of students on the shore of a lake in historic Littleton, Massachusetts. They would celebrate the nation's birthday and the end of the fast in one grand, outdoor feast.

Of course, his mother did not want him to leave. "Stay and celebrate with us," she pleaded.

"Mom, I have to go," he told her. "I organized the event. Everyone is depending on me."

As he got into the car to head to the airport, his mother stood along the street and she kept waving until she could no longer see the car.

On July 5, the fast ended and I remember I was cleaning up dishes from our own family celebration when the phone rang. It was Mohamed's sister. She screamed so loudly that I could barely understand her. I made out: "Hurry! Hurry! You have to come to our apartment." She just kept screaming until I agreed to come immediately.

When I arrived, I found chaos. And the terrible news: "Mohamed is dead!"

Eventually, we read all the news stories about the accident. Just before dinner, as the sun was about to set, Mohamed saw that the barbecue was coming along just fine. He decided to slip out onto the lake for a quick canoe trip. "Don't worry," he told people. "I'll be back right away and we'll eat."

When the sun set and Mohamed had not returned, his friends began to panic. They called the police, who found him drowned in four feet of water with his canoe tipped over. As we had expected, given his careful observance of Muslim practice, the autopsy showed no drugs or alcohol in his system. He knew how to swim, but they speculate the canoe might have struck something and flipped. We thought he might have had a seizure or perhaps the canoe hit him on the head, but the autopsy was inconclusive. It simply was one of the countless boating accidents that occur each year on our waters.

News reports were full of praise for Mohamed from leaders at his university. One story included an earlier quote from him about the importance of building strong working relationships in a community. He had said, in part, "The most valuable lesson of all is how essential teamwork is." In an ideal team, he had said, "Each individual can make a difference." That captured Mohamed's spirit and his great promise.

We found those news reports much later. At the apartment in Dearborn, on that first day, everyone was frantic. The consensus was, "We have to go out there!" I agreed to accompany his mother on what I knew as going to be a very difficult journey.

By the next day, we had seats on a flight to Boston. In the airport, everyone was so compassionate. The woman who took our baggage took extra care. In the boarding area, Mohamed's mother was obviously in shock. She wasn't crying but she could not stop pacing the floor. She's an architect and I had always been impressed by her professional presence in so many different settings. But, now, she was a mother who had lost a son and could not calm herself enough to sit down.

Because we had bought our tickets at the last moment on a holiday weekend, they were in the last row of the plane. So, we had a long walk up the aisle. The attendants were helpful, but every step, every moment, was filled with emotion. We reached the last row, where a woman in the aisle seat made room for us. Mohamed's mother sat down in the seat near the window and I took the middle seat. The other women settled into the aisle seat.

There was silence, but finally I succumbed to the overwhelming tragedy: We were going to a child's funeral! I wept. Mohamed's mother had not been crying, but now she wept. The flight attendant, without saying a word, found a box of tissues and passed them to us. She asked, "How can I help you?"

I said, "We're heading to my nephew's funeral. He was 21 and just died in a boating accident."

Now, I realized the woman on the aisle was weeping, too. She began crying even harder than we were. Her hand reached out, took my hand and finally she was able to speak, "I know just how she feels. I lost my daughter. My daughter was just 12."

"When did you lose her?" I asked.

"Seven years ago," she said. "But it is still like yesterday."

I turned to Mohamed's mother and told her, "God works in unexpected ways. This woman next to me lost her daughter when she was 12—and now here she is with us, weeping for you and your son."

Mohamed's mother looked up into my eyes. For a long moment, I held her gaze. Then, I gently took her hand and guided it across my lap. I was still holding the other woman's hand. I folded their hands together. And, that's how we flew the rest of the way to Boston. For that hour, their hands were like a reassuring seatbelt—a visible, tangible human connection holding the three of us together.

There have been many powerful stories, reminders of the way God wants us to see other people beyond all of the distinctions that can so easily distract us. God wants us to see each other's souls. And, on that heartbreaking journey, we experienced that in such a natural, organic way.

You might think of this story as exceptional, but I hope you will think of the story as quite natural. I live this story every day. My life *is* this story. We must reach out. And, when we do, we find others reaching back.

Supplements

Open My Eyes to God's Diversity

WHATEVER YOUR SPIRITUAL tradition may be, pray for us for courage, creativity and compassion in finding new friends. Pray with us for peace in the midst of God's diversity.

The following prayer-poem was written by dozens of contributors using a workshop process that you can easily adapt for your own group. You could gather participants together in a single setting. Or, if you are drawing together people from far-flung corners of the globe, you could do this virtually. Explain the process and provide an opening, prayerful phrase. In this case, we used "Open my eyes to …" Over the years, we have used other phrases, as well, including "I hope for a world where …" Participants then prayerfully reflect on completing that sentence. All responses are collected and an editor then spends time reflecting on how these many lines can flow together into a single, unified text. The result is always moving as our individual prayers and meditations become a unified voice lifting up our shared hopes and commitments.

Open my eyes to …
Peaceful things in life
Songs of peace
Seeds of understanding
Goodness in all people
The spirit of each human being I encounter today

Open my eyes to …
The world around me
Needs around me
Outer appearances that can mislead
Dangers of injustice and misunderstanding
People we need to understand
The hunger and thirst of our sisters and brothers

Open my eyes to …
The larger world
The value of women everywhere

Open my eyes to …
All the people God loves
All the species God cares about on this earth
The beauty and abundance of God's creation
The grandeur of God's creation in every person,
place and thing

Open my eyes to …
Love all around us
The face of God in those we meet
The Divine source of goodness in all peoples
The Good that is available everywhere
The power of forgiveness

Guide me so I don't stand idly by
Guide me to help according to Your will
Guide me to know the difference between what I want and what I need
Dispel the delusion that someone else is responsible for my community, my nation, my world
Open my eyes to this new day and free me from the limitations of yesterday

Open my eyes to ...
The warmth of interfaith gatherings that buildrespect and understanding
The potential in each of us to cross divides and build new friendships

Open my eyes to...
God's diversity

By the Women of WISDOM
May 2011

Acknowledgments

Acknowledgments from the 2010 edition:

The main "authors" of this book are members of WISDOM: Women's Interfaith Solutions for Dialogue and Outreach in MetroDetroit. This network of women from many religious and cultural backgrounds now has years of experience in reaching out through public service, educational efforts and cross-cultural programs—sparking widespread interest in its unique approach to peacemaking.

In January of 2009, 14 WISDOM leaders gathered for a retreat at a Muslim center in Michigan, led by the Rev. Sharon Buttry, whose story appears in this collection. The retreat was called Building Bridges and, in it, the leaders explored ways to strengthen relationships between women and create innovative projects for the future. To deepen their reflections that weekend, the women divided into pairs—and one pair consisted of Gigi Salka, a Muslim woman, and Brenda Rosenberg, a Jewish peace activist. Their bridge-building conversations were so productive that Brenda proposed expanding this process far beyond the circle of WISDOM through a book of personal stories. The group's enthusiastic response led to Brenda, Padma Kuppa, Sheri Schiff and Gail Katz forming a task force to tell their own stories—and invite dozens of women from diverse backgrounds to contribute more stories.

As that creative circle expanded, WISDOM invited writers from a similarly wide range of backgrounds to help its members tell their stories. A year-long effort unfolded in which WISDOM women spent time with these writers who interviewed them, gathered background materials, and then helped them draft their final stories. The diversity in this creative effort crosses generations. Some of the writers are still in college—and some are veteran, nationally-known writers. These co-authors include: Terry Ahwal, Kristina Birch, Amy Crumm, Debra B. Darvick, Stefanie DeHart, Stephanie Fenton, Sarah Fowlkes, Katie L. Miller, Patricia Montemurri and Frances Kai-Hwa Wang.

The WISDOM women told their stories to these writers in various forms, including taped oral histories, telephone interviews, written texts and, in some cases, archival documents and news clippings. After a co-author drafted a chapter, each woman further revised her story to make it fully her own narrative. In this almost-exclusively women's production, three men also played key roles: Artist Rick Nease designed the book cover and Web graphics; Publisher John Hile designed the book's interior and aided in the project's research; and, finally, General Editor David Crumm coordinated the work of the 40 women contributing to the project—and edited the final collection of stories.

Acknowledgments from the 2017 expanded edition:
Many women have been drawn to participate in WISDOM programs since the original edition of our signature book. So, we issued a call to expand our signature book with stories from more recent members. We anticipated a few brave souls would respond. We were overwhelmed by the dozens of women who stepped forward to write new stories of courage, creativity and compassion! Their bylines appear with their stories throughout this book and, as WISDOM's leaders, we thank each one!

This time, we organized the writing process in a new way. We already had a published model for this kind of writing. So, we began by ensuring that each new writer had a copy of our original book. We scheduled a series of writing workshops and assigned peer editors from among the many veterans in our organization to aid the new writers. Eventually, twenty-three stories emerged nearly doubling the length of the original book.

We thank our WISDOM project coordinators Trish Harris, Bobbie Lewis and the Rev. Amy Morgan for their tireless work over many months. We thank the women who stepped forward to offer assistance with peer editing and planning, including Rose Cooper, Paula Drewek, Ellen Ehrlich, Fran Hildebrandt, Karla Joy Huber, Gail Katz, Padma Kuppa and Janelle McCammon. And we thank congregations that graciously opened their doors to host our writing workshops: Christ Church Cranbrook in Bloomfield Hills, First Presbyterian Church in Birmingham and St John's Episcopal Church in Royal Oak.

Finally, we thank the many consulting readers, editors and other Front Edge Publishing professionals who assisted us, including Dmitri Barvinok, Amy Crumm, Celeste Dykas, John Hile, Rick Nease, Susan Stitt, Kathryn Szczygiel, Shaun Taft and Patty Thompson.

Become a Part of the Story! Resources and Much More

BECOME A PART of this story! Ask old friends to join you. Reach out and make new friends. As Barbara Mahany writes in this book's foreword: "We cannot afford to shrink from the task. We cannot afford to think we don't matter, that we can't make a difference. ... Be the change you believe in. Be the kindness. Be the radiant light."

As you do, please get in touch with us. Tell us what you're doing. Invite WISDOM to bring one of our programs to your community. Ask questions. To help you along this compassionate yet challenging journey, we have many online resources at our website: http://www.interfaithwisdom.com/

Among the resources we are offering:

A free discussion guide to help you plan a workshop, retreat or weekly small-group series based on this book.

A list of "Interfaith Resources" that we find helpful, including websites and online columns.

A list of recommended books.

A list of recommended films.

"HerStory," a detailed history of WISDOM through which you can learn more about the many twists, turns, challenges and opportunities that enabled our group to grow into the robust, diverse organization it is today.

A series of truths we've learned after a decade of building interfaith relationships. Some of these wise nuggets may help you to avoid pitfalls or to discern opportunities that you otherwise might miss.

Please, offer your suggestions! Some of the resources we have listed above are immediately available. Others are coming soon. Still others—such as our list of recommended web resources— will be intentionally developed step by step over the coming year. Would you like us to consider recommending your website or column or book or video to our audience? Or, perhaps you are looking for a particular resource that we have not listed here.

Please, get in touch with us through our website.

Our story grows as you join the global conversation.

Related Books

100 Questions and Answers About
Americans

This guide answers some of the first
questions asked by newcomers to the United
States. Questions represent dozens of
nationalities.

Available on Amazon.com

100 Questions and Answers About
Arab Americans

The terror attacks of Sept. 11, 2001, propelled
these Americans into a difficult position. This
guide answers basic questions to improve
cultural competence and understanding.

Available on Amazon.com

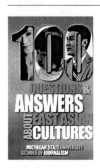

100 Questions and Answers About
East Asian Cultures

University enrollments from Asia prompted
this guide as an aid for understanding
cultural differences.

Available on Amazon.com

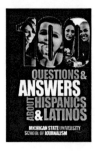

100 Questions and Answers About
Hispanics and Latinos

This group became the largest ethnic
minority in the United States in 2014.
Questions for the guide were suggested by
Hispanics and Latinos.

Available on Amazon.com

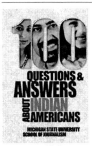

100 Questions and Answers About Indian Americans

This guide answers questions about Indian Americans. Answers also include information about Pakistanis, Bangladeshis and others groups from South Asia.

Available on Amazon.com

100 Questions, 500 Nations: A Guide to Native America

This guide about Native Americans by Michigan State University students was created in partnership with the Native American Journalists Association.

Available on Amazon.com

100 Questions and Answers About Veterans

This guide treats the more than 20 million U.S. military veterans as a cultural group with distinctive training, experiences and jargon. Graphics depict attitudes, adjustment challenges, rank, income and demographics.

Available on Amazon.com

100 Questions and Answers About Muslim Americans

This guide was written at a time of rising intolerance in the United States toward Muslims. This guide answers basic questions to improve cultural competence.

Available on Amazon.com

100 Questions and Answers About American Jews

This simple, introductory guide answers 100 of the basic questions non-Jews ask in everyday conversation.

Available on Amazon.com

100 Questions and Answers About Immigrants to the U.S.

This guide answers some of the first questions asked by newcomers to the United States. Questions represent dozens of nationalities.

Available on Amazon.com

100 Questions and Answers About African Americans

This simple, introductory guide answers 100 of the basic questions people ask about African Americans and Black people in everyday conversation.

Available on Amazon.com

United America by Wayne Baker

Dr. Wayne Baker reports a surprising truth about Americans: we are united by 10 Core Values, enabling us to rise above and see beyond political polarization.

Available on Amazon.com

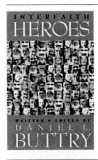

Interfaith Heroes
by Daniel L. Buttry

Interfaith Heroes showcases short biographies of men and women throughout history who crossed traditional boundaries of religious groups to build stronger communities.

Available on Amazon.com

Interfaith Heroes 2
by Daniel L. Buttry

Interfaith Heroes 2 tells even more stories of interfaith relationships and conflict resolution around the world and throughout history.

Available on Amazon.com

Blessed Are the Peacemakers
by Daniel L. Buttry

In the pages of this book, you will meet more than 100 interfaith heroes and peacemakers. Watch out! Reading about their lives may inspire you to step up into their circle.

Available on Amazon.com

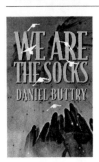

We Are the Socks
by Daniel L. Buttry

In these inspiring true stories, Buttry takes readers to some of the most dangerous and impoverished places in the world to transform conflict into peace.

Available on Amazon.com

Flavors of Faith: Holy Breads
by Lynne Golodner

Enjoy eating? Fascinated with faith? Like to share with friends? You'll love this book about timeless spiritual connections between food and faith. Includes bread recipes.

Available on Amazon.com

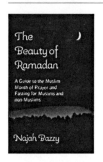

The Beauty of Ramadan
by Najah Bazzy

More than 1 billion Muslims fast in the holy month of Ramadan, revitalizing their faith and celebrating the holy Qur'an. This book is a guide to these sacred traditions.

Available on Amazon.com

Bullying Is No Laughing Matter
by Kurt Kolka

This double-sided comic book brings together a team of American's comic and cartoon favorites to fight bullying.

Available on Amazon.com

Harnessing the Power of Tension
by Brenda Rosenberg and
Samia Moustapha Bahsoun

By harnessing tension, the authors bridge their commitment as Jew and Arab to directly address the tension that separates them.

Available on Amazon.com

Access to School
by United Way for Southeastern Michigan

In this book, you will read about immigrant parents seeking a better life for their children with help from American educators.

Available on Amazon.com

Solutions for Success
by United Way for Southeastern Michigan

In this book, you'll discover an innovative program in Detroit that teaches Hispanic-immigrant parents English while ensuring their children's success at school.

Available on Amazon.com

Recess
by Laurie Haller

Laurie took a recess from her ministry and her daily life. What followed was a rejuvenating journey of reflection, recovery, and finally re-entry.

Available on Amazon.com

This Far By Faith
by Faith Fowler

Known for her deep faith and creative ideas, Faith serves as one of Detroit's leading pastors and nonprofit entrepreneurs. This memoir recounts her incredible efforts.

Available on Amazon.com

9 781942 011934

CPSIA inform
at www.ICGt
Printed in the
FFOW03n165
40677FF